How to Detect Developmental Delay and
What to
Do Next

of related interest

Understanding Nonverbal Learning Disabilities
A Common-Sense Guide for Parents and Professionals
Maggie Mamen
ISBN 978 1 84310 593 0
JKP Essentials series

Understanding Motor Skills in Children with Dyspraxia, ADHD, Autism, and Other Learning Disabilities
A Guide to Improving Coordination
Lisa A. Kurtz
ISBN 978 1 84310 865 8

Understanding Your Young Child with Special Needs
Pamela Bartram
ISBN 978 1 84310 533 6
The Tavistock Clinic – Understanding Your Child series

Mary Mountstephen

How to Detect Developmental Delay and What to Do Next

Practical Interventions for Home and School

Jessica Kingsley *Publishers*
London and Philadelphia

Information about primitive reflexes on pp.25–31 is adapted with the kind permission of Sally Goddard Blythe and Jill Christmas.
Section on movement programmes on pp.72–4 is adapted with the kind permission of Barbara Pheloung.
Drawings on pp.82–3 reprinted from *Miracle Children* © 2008, Anna R. Buck. Used by permission.
Permission for the reproduction of the list of indications of dyslexia in Chapter 3 is kindly provided by the British Dyslexia Association.
Permission for the reproduction of the list of symptoms of dyspraxia in Chapter 3 is kindly provided by the Dyspraxia Foundation.
'Why we should be interested in behavioural optometry' section in Chapter 5 © Christopher Young 2010.
Vision checklist in Chapter 5 reproduced with the kind permission of Ian Jordan.
Leaflet about behavioural optometry in Chapter 5 reproduced with the kind permission of Philippa Bodien.
'Sound therapy and auditory stimulation programmes' section in Chapter 6 has been kindly contributed by Camilla Leslie and Diana Crewdson.
Chapter 7, 'How a Psychologist Can Help', has been kindly contributed by Elvie Brown.
CAPD leaflet in Appendix III reproduced with the kind permission of Julia Kidd and Nerys Roberts.

First published in 2011
by Jessica Kingsley Publishers
116 Pentonville Road
London N1 9JB, UK
and
400 Market Street, Suite 400
Philadelphia, PA 19106, USA

www.jkp.com

Library of Congress Cataloging in Publication Data
A CIP catalog record for this book is available from the Library of Congress

British Library Cataloguing in Publication Data
A CIP catalogue record for this book is available from the British Library

ISBN 978 1 84905 022 7

Printed and bound in Great Britain by
MPG Books Group

This book is dedicated to my parents, for
giving me every opportunity to thrive

Acknowledgements

I would like to thank the following:

My colleagues in the Learning Development Centre for their daily hard work, dedication and commitment to nurturing the independent learning spirit.

My editor and production editor, Lisa Clark and Victoria Peters, for their patience.

Peter Blythe, Sally Goddard Blythe, Elvie Brown, Ian Jordan, Barbara Pheloung, Christopher Young, Camilla Leslie and Diana Crewdson for their advice, time and valued contributions.

Contents

Notes from the Author

This book is aimed primarily at parents, carers and teachers who are living or working with children of primary-school age. It will also be of relevance for those who are concerned about the progress and achievements of older children.

I have included checklists and other information which is intended for guidance only, not for diagnosis. In the first instance, parents or carers should look to speaking with their child's school or seeking medical advice from their family doctor.

Throughout this book, the term 'parent/parents' should be taken to include other family members such as grandparents and carers. The terms girl, boy and his or hers and so on will be used interchangeably unless otherwise indicated.

The children in this book are composites of many children. The descriptions of them create a picture of the type of learning and behaviour which illustrates certain points. It is important to remember that each child is an individual, that each child is unique and has his own developmental profile.

The most important message of this book is that you can make a difference if you know where to look. There are many reasons why children fail to thrive and in this book I have only scratched the surface. There are specialists such as occupational therapists, speech and language therapists and others whose knowledge is far superior to mine and I apologize in advance for my limitations.

Introduction

'Anna's just the way she is…there's nothing to worry about… she'll get there in her own time.'

'Kyle won't listen in class, he won't sit still, he wriggles all the time and he distracts other children.'

'Max just doesn't pay attention…he is such a nuisance!'

'We know Toby has hearing problems and we are trying to help him in the classroom, but he does need to try and concentrate more and avoid being distracted.'

'I'm fed up with them not listening to me. Gemma's a bright little button but she hates reading and her homework takes us hours. Her school doesn't seem to know what to do to help her…'

Every child has a unique cluster of physical, mental and emotional challenges to overcome combined with strengths, interests and talents which may never fully develop if they are unrecognized. I wrote this book, in collaboration with colleagues, so that teachers, parents and others concerned about a child's progress could find out more about factors which may be contributing to her difficulties. As the child's parent or teacher, you may have a gut feeling that she is not doing as well as she should be in class or when compared to other children. Frustration, poor behaviour, erratic performance or emotional outbursts can be outward signs of underlying and unidentified difficulties. A lack of awareness can mean that children tolerate, and are tolerated in, schools throughout their education with invisible disabilities which are unrecognized. Children with such unrecognized difficulties often under-achieve academically, lose faith in themselves and come to accept the judgements others have made about them and their potential. These are often the children who do not have a 'diagnosis' of dyslexia, dyspraxia, specific learning difficulty, ADHD or any other condition, but are often unhappy, unmotivated and under-achieving. Their behaviours and achievements are dependent on the underlying and invisible atypical activity taking place all the time in their bodies and in their nervous systems and this is rarely taken into account as it is not widely understood or acknowledged. Learning difficulties often go unrecognized as bright children, for example, learn strategies to adapt and to cope. They do make progress, but these strategies may not be helping them to learn as effectively as they might.

This book will introduce you to information which can help a child at home, in the classroom, playground and in her daily life. Sometimes parents feel that their concerns are not being taken seriously by school or by other professionals and they are anxious that time is passing fast and once gone, can never be retrieved. As a general rule, we believe that parents know their child better than anyone else and their gut reactions about their child need to be taken seriously. The fact is, however, that these concerns are more likely to be listened to if they are supported with evidence or documentation and if parents or teachers have a road map they can follow to help them make appropriate decisions. Parents' concerns are often accurate indicators of the child's underlying developmental problems and the key to helping a child is the ability to identify the most appropriate forms of supports and strategies which can be put in place. The child you are concerned about may get there in her own time: but what are the consequences in the meantime and what happens if she continues to fall behind?

Jill Christmas, a respected occupational therapist, believes that understanding and sharing what the issues are can make a real difference to the child, the family and the school. 'If we can understand some of the underlying sensory/motor influences and their impact on function in everyday living, we can then more easily support these children, their carers, teachers and other professionals in facilitating each child's best level of output' (Christmas 2009, p.1). She explains that some children can be wrongly labelled as 'lazy' or 'awkward' when their underlying difficulties are unrecognized.

What are the possible reasons for what we see in the classroom?

- Anna doesn't raise alarm bells in school and she just seems a little slow in terms of other children of the same age. I hope this book might help you to identify whether Anna needs extra support to thrive.

- One of the reasons Kyle might be a 'wriggler' is that he has sensory problems that are causing him to be constantly on the move.

- Max doesn't pay attention because he is easily distracted by sounds and movement and he struggles to communicate effectively, so he switches off.

- Toby's teacher thinks his mother is making too much of his hearing difficulties. He thinks Toby, aged 10, is using his hearing difficulties as a way to avoid work and that he is lazy. Toby has an educational psychology assessment that says he is bright, so he should be doing much better than he is. Is his hearing or the school's approach, or a combination of the two, responsible for his under-performance?

- Gemma and her mother have daily battles over reading. She is a little girl who causes no problems in a busy classroom. She wants to please, so she tries hard and can't understand why it seems so much easier for everyone else and why she always finishes last.

This book reveals why these children and others might be behaving as they are and provides strategies that will help them and others like them at home and at school. If you are concerned about the lack of progress a child is making and want to know more about why and how you can help, read on.

The author's background

Over the years I have worked in many schools for children with a wide range of difficulties. This has included two headships of schools with nurseries, where I taught across the age range and served for a period as special educational needs coordinator (SENCO). I have also taught in schools where all the children had been identified as having social, emotional and behavioural problems and schools where all pupils had moderate learning difficulties.

In all of these schools there were children who were failing to thrive and ultimately failing to be as responsive, motivated and successful as every child deserves to be. In my experience these are the sort of children who sometimes disappoint their parents, their teachers and often themselves. This book also draws on my experiences as the parent of two children, now successful adults who I am very proud of.

What do children and young people need to thrive?

Victoria Climbié, an eight-year-old British child, died in February 2000 of injuries sustained after months of abuse at the hands of her great aunt Marie-Theresa Kouao and her boyfriend Carl Manning. The report that followed her death blamed a gross failure of the British system of public agencies responsible for protecting vulnerable children from deliberate harm. It contained many recommendations for fundamental changes to the way British social care, healthcare and police child protection services are organized and managed at national and local level, in order to establish a clear line of accountability in the provision of services for vulnerable children and the support of families.

The message of this report has universal significance. In order to thrive, a child must:

- be healthy
- stay safe
- enjoy and achieve
- make a positive contribution
- achieve economic well-being.

What does this mean for schools? Schools and teachers have a role in making sure that every child can make the best of their learning experience by working closely with, for example, local health services, social services and other local agencies. Because of the amount of contact time children have with schools they are central to the integration of all children's services, and to development of a common understanding of what children need and who can provide it.

Evidence shows that parental involvement in children's education has a significant positive effect on educational achievement, not just early on in life, but also into adolescence and adulthood. It is encouraging that the most important steps parents and carers can take to support learning are quite simple, for example, talking to their child every day and showing a daily interest in their child's learning at school. Schools have an important role to play, particularly in encouraging parents and carers to keep track of their children's progress, and keeping them well informed about how else they can help. Education should be a shared partnership and responsibility among pupils, schools and parents, with clear understanding about expectations and how success can be achieved through working together.

This is a practical guide for anyone who wants to be more tuned in to the factors which can render a child less effective than she might be in any aspect of her development. I am passionate about helping children to experience success: as an individual right, but also for their potential in making valuable contributions to society. I see adults who are frustrated because they are not able to get the kind of work they would like; their horizons have been limited by their early experiences. If this book helps you have a better understanding of where your child is, and what you can do to help her to 'thrive', it is possible that you will be making an unforgettable and fundamental shift in her life's direction. Early support can nurture efficient learning and intervening early can increase cognitive flexibility, resilience and mental well-being.

Too many children end up in unchallenging jobs and disenchanted with life because the symptoms of their difficulties were the focus of attention – rather than the causes.

I have written this book to help you to become more knowledgeable about what might or might not underlie your concern and to provide practical information about what actions can be taken. It will support you in understanding:

- what to expect at certain stages of child development

- how you can begin to identify areas of strength and weakness in a child and why these might be present – looking for the clues

- where to go for support and why

- what the roles of various professionals are

- what you can do yourself to help a child to thrive

- school-based and home-based strategies and interventions you can put into action.

The first part of this book is an introduction to child development and covers some of the difficulties that children might experience and suggests how parents and teachers can learn about these. In the second part each chapter focuses on a particular area or aspect and includes checklists and guidance for the reader.

Chapter 4, 'Movement and Learning', looks at what might be causing some of a child's problems and how they may be helped.

In Chapter 5, 'Vision, Visual Processing and Learning', there are insights from two professionals working in this field, Chris Young and Ian Jordan, who explain why vision is not all about 20/20 vision.

Experienced speech and language therapists, Camilla Leslie and Diana Crewdson, have contributed to Chapter 6 to provide a perspective on the impact that hearing and listening problems have on learning.

The role of the educational psychologist is described in Chapter 7 by independent educational psychologist Elvie Brown. She explains how and why children may need to see her and what to expect.

In the appendices you will find further sources of information which can be of help in areas such as dyslexia and dyspraxia, as well as examples of hearing and listening programmes.

Part I:

Child Development and Signs of Delay

1

Factors Affecting Early Development

This chapter looks at:

★ pregnancy and child development

★ genetic and environmental factors

★ the role of primitive and postural reflexes.

Pregnancy and early brain development

The brain has evolved over hundreds of millions of years to be a very complex collection or community of structures. Each part of the brain has specialized functions but all parts work in unison to help us adapt to and survive in our environment. At birth the brain is equipped with more than 100 billion nerve cells or neurons that communicate through tiny connections that form networks. These networks are connected into systems which work together to carry out a set of specific functions such as vision and hearing. These mental systems are designed to sense, process and store information received both from the outside word and from inside the body (for example hunger, pain and emotions).

During pregnancy, the basic structure of the brain is formed, beginning at sixteen days after conception. Within seven months the brain transforms from a small group of cells to a highly complex organism that has the form, if not the function, of the mature brain. The different areas are in place and the basic brain functions that help the baby to survive are established. Unlike the heart and other organs of the body which are already functioning much as they will throughout life, the brain is immature and goes through many changes. Newborn infants function on only a very small part of the brain called the brain stem which deals with all the basic functions you need to stay alive such as breathing. Curran, in his fascinating and very readable book *The Little Book of Big Stuff about the Brain* (2008), describes the newborn baby's brain as a:

> clean slate ready to receive new learning. Other than a few primitive reflexes that seem to be genetically determined and reside in the brainstem, newborn babies have no stored templates. (p.129)

It is as the brain develops that the different areas become fully mature according to a pre-determined biological timing. At birth, the brain stem is fully working, whereas the higher order functions mature later, with brain development continuing into young adulthood.

The brain not only grows and changes as a function of development (Couperous and Nelson 2008), but it also continually interacts with itself and the environment, adapting to achieve the best level of functioning. This ongoing adaptation is termed 'plasticity' and refers to the brain's ability to change and adapt in response to changes in the brain or the environment. Learning is highly dependent on the experiences we have and while all typically developing children are capable, for example, of learning how to make biscuits, not all children do. The specific learning which takes place in our brains depends on how the brain is assembled, genetic influences and other factors and experiences such as those below.

Genetic influences on development

People often say that learning difficulties run in families, particularly when children seem to be experiencing the same problems as another family member. However, a parent's learning difficulty or difference may not take exactly the same form as her child's. Some learning differences such as dyslexia often do seem to run in families and it is known that in many cases genes do play an important role. It is not uncommon to find that multiple members of an immediate or extended family have dyslexia. Family studies of dyslexia indicate that almost 50 per cent of children born to a parent with dyslexia will end up facing difficulties in the acquisition of reading skill (Lyytinen *et al.* 2008, p.122). In addition between 30 and 50 per cent of the brothers and sisters of a child with dyslexia may themselves have dyslexia – but genes are not the only factor influencing its occurrence. If dyslexia were completely genetic, we would expect that identical twins (who share the same genes) would always share dyslexia if present, but in only about 70 per cent of affected cases are both members of an identifiable twin pair dyslexic (Molfese *et al.* 2008).

Smoking, alcohol and other drug use in pregnancy

Lise Eliot, in her book *What's Going on in There? How the Brain and Mind Develop in the First Five Years of Life* (1999), has provided an excellent guide to the brain's development through the first five years of life.

She details the difficulties which cigarettes, illegal drugs, caffeine can cause and points out that these represent a continuum from devastating effects on the foetus to subtler long-term effects, including the slower development of sensory, motor or language abilities as well as disorders of attention, sleep and poor academic achievement. Characterized as neurodevelopmental disorders, these can cause parents to be concerned about their child's progress in relation to other children of the same age.

Prematurity

Prematurity is defined as childbirth occurring earlier than 37 weeks of gestation. The earlier a baby is born, the greater are the risks of physical complications, periods of separation from the mother and a restricted level of sensory stimulation in terms of movement experience, feeding and touch.

Pre-term children have a normal range of intelligence, however, difficulties such as language delay, attention deficit, hyperactivity and behaviour problems have been identified as associated with prematurity.

When these children reach school, they are more prone to weaknesses in communication skills, maths reasoning, reading comprehension and other areas of the curriculum (Allen 1996). Children who are born prematurely can be 9–12 months developmentally behind other children of the same age and the brains of premature boys are more severely affected than the brains of premature girls (Sousa 2007).

Although premature babies do make up for lost time in achieving their developmental milestones, they remain at a disadvantage as they are expected to enter school and function based on their birth date, rather than their *expected* birth date. The implications of prematurity can be long lasting, for example:

> A child who is born at 32 weeks in July or August is not only going to be one of the youngest in the school year based on birth date, but if school entry were to be based on *expected* date of birth, the child would be placed in the *next* school year, allowing a margin of a further ten months to make up for time lost in the womb, and for time spent fighting for life in the first weeks after birth. In the first five years of life when neurological development takes place at a rapid rate, the difference of a month in development can be the equivalent of a year, two decades later. (Goddard Blythe 2009, p.186)

Stress during pregnancy

Although post-natal depression is a well-known condition, prenatal depression is more common and at least as damaging to the child, according to Vivette Glover, a professor of perinatal psychobiology. Women's stress levels reach the growing baby on a physical level. Maternal anxiety affects the placenta, reducing the activity of the barrier enzyme that hinders the stress hormone cortisol from reaching the foetus (Glover 2002). This, in turn, has an impact on foetal brain development, a phenomenon that has been clearly demonstrated in animals. A baby born to a mother who has suffered extreme stress during pregnancy could behave like a miniature stressed adult after birth, being more prone to crying, fretting, sleep disturbances, feeding problems and hypersensitivity (Goddard Blythe 2009).

Fear, stress and anxiety are all very useful emotions, which have evolved over millions of years to allow us to respond quickly and efficiently to threatening situations. But problems can arise when mothers are unduly stressed during pregnancy, or are very anxious personality types. Eliot (1999) writes of evidence that prenatal stress interferes with foetal and newborn brain function with possible links to delays in mental and motor development.

Family life, nutrition, technology and communication

Inheriting a genetic *tendency* for a learning problem does not necessarily mean that it will manifest. The environment is all-important, exerting a powerful influence in determining whether certain genetic traits arise and come to affect one's behaviour and learning (for more on this see Sousa 2007). It has always been the case that some children are brought up in environments where there are many pressures that can have a significant impact on how well they develop. It is commonly accepted, however, that the rate of change in society means that families often spend less time in each other's company as traditions such as eating a family meal together are in decline and technology has replaced conversation in many households. Sue Palmer, in her book *21st Century Boys* (Palmer 2009) writes about her findings in relation to the life experiences of too many children in modern society. She brings together research showing how factors such as junk food, poor sleeping patterns, a screen-based lifestyle with little exercise, family fragmentation and the effects of consumer culture can affect children's development. What she also found was that boys are more affected by this than girls and that boys are at greater risk of developmental disorders such as ADHD (attention deficit hyperactivity disorder), dyspraxia (problems with coordination) and dyslexia.

Poor diet and lack of exercise are often linked to sleep problems and these in turn are often associated with learning and behavioural problems. Obesity is increasing around the world and in all categories. Chances are great that obese children will remain obese into adulthood and the increase in obesity is linked to diets high in fat and sugar. Food and diet are important to all of us at the most fundamental level. Without the right nutrients, it simply isn't possible for our brains and bodies to develop properly and to function properly. Alex Richardson (2006) maintains that there is evidence that poor nutrition is putting children's physical health at risk and suggests, controversially and shockingly, that many children are now expected to die before their parents, as a direct result of their unhealthy diets and lifestyles. In her book *They Are What You Feed Them*, she covers practical issues relating to diet and how changes in lifestyle and diet can have a positive impact on a child's IQ, and help with some of the issues relating to dyslexia, attention and hyperactivity. There are a number of ways in which parents can support children nutritionally. For example, as Elvie Brown points out later in her chapter on the role of the educational psychologist, many children with ADHD characteristics can be helped by eating slow release carbohydrate foods such as whole grain breads and crackers, potatoes with their skin, beans and legumes, brown rice, oats and whole grain pasta. Fruit is an excellent snack. Eating fruit will sustain energy for longer, for example, than fruit juice, which provides the body with a quick release of fruit sugar into the bloodstream.

Children get on average one and a half hour's less sleep per night than required for healthy physical and mental development. TV and computer games are cited as the main culprit, speeding up mental processing, creating a state of 'heightened awareness' which prevents children from falling asleep naturally (Palmer 2007). One neuroscience educator classifies the songs, movement and musical games of childhood as 'brilliant neurological exercises' that introduce children to speech patterns, develop their sensory motor skills, and enable them to learn vital movement strategies. The spontaneous transmission of this playful 'brain training' is being replaced by TV, work, and even the more academic approach that some early childhood programmes are taking (Coulter 1995). Children are surrounded by media and technology which compete for their attention and at the same time they have less access to physical exercise at school and are more house-bound as parents fear for their safety outside in the neighbourhood. As they miss outdoor opportunities to develop their physical skills and their social skills, they play less with other children, communicate less with other members of the family and have difficulty focusing for extended periods. They are easily distracted and they fail to learn the negotiation and listening skills they need to function as a group member.

A child with a genetic profile pre-disposing him to language problems, who lives in a home where there is little high quality interactive communication, is likely to display symptoms of this problem from an early age, whereas if he is born into a family where there is frequent high quality communication and interaction, it is less likely that language problems will emerge. If language problems do arise, it is more likely in this sort of environment that they will become more established as academic demands outstrip his coping mechanisms.

Primitive and postural reflexes

Several years ago, my longstanding interest in the role of movement led me to attend a one day teacher training course with the Institute of Neuro-Physiological Psychology. This inspired me so much that I went on to study on their full training course in neurodevelopmental delay. The following information comes from the course I undertook with Sally Goddard Blythe.

There are three main categories of reflexes:

1. Intra-uterine reflexes that appear and are suppressed during intra-uterine development (i.e. not present at birth).

2. Intra-uterine, birth or *primitive* reflexes: these appear during later intra-uterine development, are present at birth and are inhibited by around six months of age.

3. *Postural* reflexes that appear during late infancy following inhibition of the primitive reflexes.

A human baby comes into the world with a number of *primitive* reflexes, which contribute in various ways to its birth, survival and subsequent development. These include grasping, sucking and turning the head when touched near the mouth. An understanding of how these reflexes work and change as the infant develops is essential to our comprehension of early child development. Each primitive reflex has either to be inhibited or transformed in the course of a baby's normal interaction with his environment, so allowing his brain to release, in chronological sequence, a series of *postural* reflexes (e.g. the head-righting reflexes), to give him control of his sensory body within the environment and so that he develops the ability to manipulate that environment. Primitive reflexes are *automatic*.

> They are stereotyped movements, directed from the brain stem and executed without cortical control. They are essential for the baby's survival in the first weeks of life and provide basic training for many later voluntary skills. However, these primitive reflexes should only have a limited life-span and should in time be inhibited or controlled by higher centres of the brain if they are not to become 'aberrant' that is, still active beyond 6–12 months of life. (Goddard Blythe 2002)

Peter Blythe and Sally Goddard Blythe have written extensively about the role primitive and postural reflexes play in a child's development. In her book *The Well-Balanced Child* (2004), Goddard Blythe has produced an excellent introduction to this field. Jill Christmas's book, *Hands on Dyspraxia* (2009) also has a very readable section on the impact that retained reflexes can have on a child's development.

The continued presence of primitive reflexes beyond this age is seen as evidence of structural weaknesses or immaturity within the brain – Central Nervous System – and succeeding vital postural reflexes may not develop as a result. Without this natural progression from primitive to more sophisticated postural reflexes, 'it is as if the acquisition of later skills remains tethered to an earlier stage of development and instead of becoming automatic, can only be mastered through continuous conscious effort' (Goddard Blythe 2002).

A baby's reflex profile can also provide indicators of possible future problems such as:

- postural control
- balance
- motor skills
- learning
- emotional functioning.

Some key primitive reflexes

The information about the following reflexes is adapted with the kind permission of Goddard Blythe (2002) and Christmas (2009).

The Moro reflex

The Moro reflex (also known as 'the startle reflex') functions as the primitive alerting mechanism to stress for the foetus: in this reflex, the arms fling outwards with open hands, resulting in stimulation of the sympathetic nervous system. Symptoms of this stimulation include:

- increase in heart rate

- immediate rise in blood pressure

- rapid shallow breathing

- flushing of the face

- anger or distress.

A fully or partially retained Moro reflex or failure to inhibit the Moro reflex is often a factor in symptoms and disorders which are associated with enervation of the sympathetic nervous system: anxiety, panic disorder, hormonal problems, poor immunity or over-active immune system, allergies.

If the Moro reflex has only been partially inhibited as the baby develops you may see evidence in the developing child of:

- defensive 'body armouring' in an attempt to control the retained tendency to over-reaction through muscular tension

- vestibular related problems such as motion sickness, poor balance and coordination, hypersensitivity to vestibular stimulation

- oculo-motor and visual perceptual problems

- hypersensitivity to sound

- low self-esteem, weak ego or insecurity

- need to control or manipulate events

- hyperactivity or excessive fatigue.

The tonic labyrinthine reflex

The tonic labyrinthine reflex (TLR) begins to develop from 12 weeks after conception. It is involved with the vestibular system in the inner ear and helps in the development of a sense of balance. It also interacts with the other senses. The TLR presents as a primitive response to gravity and relates to flexor and extensor muscular tone.

If this reflex is only partially inhibited or if it is retained there may the following signs:

- postural instability (e.g. problems with head movement forwards and backwards)
- balance and muscle tone weaknesses
- difficulty in judging space, distance, depth and velocity
- vestibular-ocular reflex problems
- head-righting problems
- vertigo
- motion sickness
- orientation problems
- auditory problems (e.g. difficulty separating out foreground and background noise).

Asymmetric tonic neck reflex

The asymmetric tonic neck reflex (ATNR) is an automatic whole body movement pattern and is observed by turning a baby's head to one side.

> A 'fencing' or 'archery' posture can be observed in a small baby. It is elicited when the baby turns their head to one side – the arm and leg on that side stretch out and extend while the opposite arm and leg flex (bend). The opposite pattern occurs when the baby turns its head to face the other way. (Christmas 2009, p.120)

The ATNR functions to:

- facilitate movement in utero

- develop muscle tone
- provide vestibular stimulation
- develop homolateral movement
- assist in birth process
- ensure free airway when lying prone
- facilitate early hand–eye training.

If only partially inhibited or if retained, this reflex can lead to problems with:

- balance when the head is rotated
- crossing the midline (i.e. the ability to move hand, foot and eyes across the centre of the body)
- writing: hand–eye coordination
- hand–eye coordination (tracking)
- horizontal eye movements (tracking)
- bilateral integration (i.e. the ability to coordinate both sides of the body together effectively as well as the upper and lower body)
- cross laterality (favouring different hands for various tasks) above the age of eight years.

The spinal galant reflex

According to Goddard Blythe:

> Little is known about the functions of the spinal Galant reflex, except that it may take an active role in the birth process. Contractions of the vaginal wall stimulate the lumbar region and cause small rotational movements of the hip on one side, similar to the head and shoulder movements of the asymmetrical tonic neck reflex. In this way, the baby can help to work its way down the birth canal. (Goddard Blythe 2002, p.16)

The spinal galant reflex functions to:

- facilitate movement in utero

- promote hip flexibility

- may act as a primitive conductor of sound in utero, allowing sound vibration to travel up through the body.

If only partially inhibited or if retained, this reflex leads to problems such as the following:

- an 'ants in the pants' child (who may benefit from wriggle cushions)

- poor concentration and communication

- bedwetting

- issues of tactile sensitivity

- problems with auditory processing

- a possible connection to soiling in older children.

The rooting and sucking reflex

Searching, sucking and swallowing reflexes should be present in all full-term newborn babies. They also form part of the group of 'grasp' reflexes which develop in utero. The functions of the rooting and sucking reflex are:

- searching (rooting) suck reflex

- swallowing (suck) reflex.

The response to touch that results in the above reflexes eventually transfers from a tactile to a visual response – the sight of the breast will stimulate feeding movements. This reflex may also help to develop the muscle groups involved in smiling and speech.

If only partially inhibited or if retained, this reflex results in:

- continued sensitivity and immature responses to touch in the mouth region (particularly the lip)

- difficulty when solid foods are introduced (problems with chewing and swallowing)
- dribbling continuing into school age
- problems with speech and articulation
- difficulty with manual dexterity.

Post-natal postural reflexes
The symmetrical tonic neck reflex
This reflex:

- helps the baby to get up off the floor onto his hands and knees from the prone position
- is a bridging reflex which forms a bridge to the next stage of movement.

Possible problems with the persistence of this reflex may include:

- poor posture: children slump when sitting
- a Simian walk
- taking up a W position when sitting on floor: children can't or won't sit cross-legged
- problems with hand–eye coordination
- messy eating and clumsiness
- difficulties with readjustment of binocular vision
- slowness at copying tasks
- difficulty learning to swim
- attention difficulties related to sitting in one position
- slumping over their desk with their legs extended, or tucking one leg underneath
- difficulties with vertical tracking (e.g. in maths).

The Landau reflex

Between three and four months the Landau reflex emerges. 'When the infant is held under the stomach in a horizontal prone position, the infant will respond by extending the head and trunk' (Goddard Blythe 2009, p.149). The Landau reflex functions as a bridging reflex which has an inhibitory effect on the tonic labyrinthine reflex and helps to develop extensor tone.

The continued presence of the Landau reflex in later life suggests underlying primitive reflex activity, particularly retention of the TLR, and this can affect the following:

- the development of balance

- may cause the child to run with stiff awkward movement in the lower part of his body

- lead to difficulty with hopping, skipping and jumping.

(Goddard Blythe 2002, p.34)

The head-righting reflexes

The results of failure of the head-righting reflexes to develop fully include possible impairment of balance, controlled eye movements and visual perception. Muscle tension in the shoulder or neck, combined with poor posture may also be a result of under-developed head-righting reflexes.

The combined effects of immature reflexes in development

Retained primitive reflexes can underlie difficulties in the learning of basic skills such as reading, writing and copying and may be at the root of many disorders of developmental delay.

> The effect of under-developed post-natal or postural reflexes in a child is the environmental and social equivalent of having an under-developed vocabulary. Often an individual can cope as long as the rules remain the same and it is possible to use previously learned skills. If the rules required by a situation

change, such children are forced to 'learn and practice' the new rules because they are not able to adapt and change to meet the altered circumstances. This can result in 'awkwardness', feelings of personal and social inadequacy and increased propensity to suffer from anxiety. (Goddard Blythe 2002, p.37)

Summary

Children who are causing concern at home or in school may be doing so for a number of reasons which are not directly linked to their ability. These can include genetic factors, issues related to the pregnancy, social and environmental factors and physical factors such as the impact of problems with primitive and postural reflexes. By looking at the causes of difficulties rather than the observable symptoms, it becomes possible to work out strategies and solutions which can have a significant impact on how well a child is able to learn, achieve and thrive.

What to Expect in the Early Years

This chapter looks at:

★ what developmental milestones are

★ how they help in the identification of possible problems

★ when you should start to be concerned and initial action that can be taken.

The first years of life are crucial to the future development of the child and of the adult the child will become. As the infant develops skills of perception, movement and the processing of information, the experiences which she has will impact fundamentally on her rate of and quality of development. The period from birth to age seven is a time when each child is making huge strides in terms of development, although this will be unique to each child in terms of how she progresses through the pre-determined developmental sequence. There are wide variations between the times at which children meet accepted milestones and, for example, a child whose physical skills are well developed may not be as well developed in terms of academic learning, relating to others or coping emotionally.

HOW WELL IS ROSIE DOING?

Rosie is coming up to four years old. She loves going to dancing class at the weekends with her mother. She confidently joins in a circle with a large group of children without the need to run back to her mother for reassurance. She has good balance and can copy tapping, tip toeing, spinning and simple dances set to nursery rhymes. She plays happily with other children at nursery and shows affection towards other children. If they fall over, she would help them and ask 'You all right?' When out shopping with Mummy, she likes to talk with the person on the till. She loves pretend play. Rosie is the 'baby bunny' and her mother is the 'mummy bunny'. Rosie will only put on her shoes when addressed as 'baby bunny' when she is playing this game. Where Rosie is less advanced developmentally though, is in skills such as writing and mark making. She is not interested in learning to recognize her name card at nursery although many other children in her group do so. This does not mean that Rosie is gifted in some aspects and delayed in others; it means that her developmental profile, at this moment in time, shows that some skills are more developed than others. It is most likely that her development will proceed towards greater complexity and organization as she acquires hands-on learning experiences, and encounters challenges and choices, but it is possible that she will have delays which need to be recognized and monitored to avoid longer-term issues.

Developmental milestones

Skills such as taking a first step, smiling for the first time and waving and saying 'bye bye' are called developmental milestones. For example, babies are generally expected to be mobile (rolling, crawling, bottom-shuffling or walking) by the time they reach their first birthday. Knowledge of these patterns of expected development helps health visitors and doctors to look at the child as a whole and to measure her progress against others of the same age. Milestones are landmarks or turning points in an individual's development, with each skill having a preceding milestone associated with it. For example:

- to walk, you must be able to stand

- to stand, you must be able to hold yourself upright

- to hold yourself upright, you must be able to hold your head erect.

Children can be measured in terms of their progress against these milestones in all areas of their development including playing, learning, communicating, behaving and moving (crawling and walking for example). Children develop at their own pace, so it is not possible to tell exactly when a child will learn a given skill. Developmental milestones give parents and professionals a general idea of the changes that can be expected as the child grows and they can act as warning indicators or hazard lights if her progress does not seem to be taking place within the generally expected time-frames. The developmental progress of a child can also vary according to the area of development: a child may be making very good progress with milestones relating to physical development, such as walking and running, but the same child may not be advanced in their hand and fine motor skills and may show little interest in printing letters.

Examples of developmental milestones

There are some skills that most children of the same age will have mastered. The milestones have been determined by looking at large groups of children's development and considering what the 'norm' for each age is (Beaver *et al.* 1994; Meggitt 2006). This means there will always be some variation, with some children performing in advance of the milestones. Please note that these are guidelines only.

Developmental milestones at two to three years old
MOVING AROUND (GROSS MOTOR SKILLS)

- Can climb nursery apparatus.
- Can jump with both feet together.
- Can kick a large ball, but with limited power and control.

USING MY HANDS (FINE MOTOR SKILLS)

- Can draw circles, lines and dots with preferred hand.
- Can build a tower with seven blocks, with a greater attention span.
- Can drink from a cup with fewer spills and manage scooping with a spoon at mealtimes.

LANGUAGE AND COMMUNICATION

- Can talk clearly and understandably to herself when playing.
- Can use 'I', 'me' and 'you' correctly.

At three to four years old
MOVING AROUND (GROSS MOTOR SKILLS)

- Can stand and walk on tip toe.
- Can walk in different directions.
- Can kick a ball.
- Can walk upstairs with one foot at a time and downstairs with two feet on each step.
- Can use pedals on a tricycle.

USING MY HANDS (FINE MOTOR SKILLS)

- Can build a tower with nine or ten bricks.
- Can place small objects in a small opening.
- Can cut with scissors, and copy a circle.
- Can dress herself, only requiring assistance with laces, buttons, and other fasteners in awkward places.

LANGUAGE AND COMMUNICATION

- Has a vocabulary of many hundreds of words.
- Composes sentences of three to four words.
- Frequently asks questions.

At four to five years old
MOVING AROUND (GROSS MOTOR SKILLS)

- Can stand on one foot for ten seconds or longer.
- Can stand, walk and run on tip toe.

- Can hop, climb.
- Can walk or run upstairs and downstairs, putting one foot on each step.
- Can control a tricycle well, making confident turns.

USING MY HANDS (FINE MOTOR SKILLS)

- Can build a tower of ten or more bricks.
- Can hold a pencil with a steady three-finger grip.
- Draws a person with head, legs and body.
- Dresses and undresses without assistance.

LANGUAGE AND COMMUNICATION

- Recalls parts of a story.
- Speaks in sentences of more than five words.
- Tells longer stories.

At five to six years old

MOVING AROUND (GROSS MOTOR SKILLS)

- Can walk on a balance beam.
- May be able to skip.
- Is getting better at running and jumping and playing ball games.
- Can catch balls with her hands.

USING MY HANDS (FINE MOTOR SKILLS)

- Can copy a series of blocks to make a staircase of one to four blocks.
- Can hold a pencil or paintbrush with a steady three-finger grip.

- Draws a person with head, legs and body and eyes, nose and mouth.

- Can thread a large needle and sew stitches.

LANGUAGE AND COMMUNICATION

- Can listen carefully.

- Is talkative and uses longer sentences.

- Enjoys teaching others – let her be the teacher and you the learner.

- By the age of six, children with average development will know the meaning of between 10,000 and 13,000 words.

At six to seven years old

MOVING AROUND (GROSS MOTOR SKILLS)

- Can jump off apparatus in school or at park with confidence.

- Can catch and throw balls with accuracy.

- Can skip in time to music.

- Can kick a football up to 6 metres (18 feet).

USING MY HANDS (FINE MOTOR SKILLS)

- Can build a tower of cubes that is virtually straight.

- Can hold a pencil in standard grip (the dynamic tripod grasp).

- Can control the size of the letters she writes.

- Draws recognizable man, tree, house.

- Colours inside lines.

LANGUAGE AND COMMUNICATION

- Can talk fluently and with confidence.

- Can remember and repeat songs.

- Uses increasingly more complex descriptions.

At seven to eight years old
MOVING AROUND (GROSS MOTOR SKILLS)

- Hops, skips and jumps confidently.
- Chases and dodges others.
- Can ride a bicycle without stabilizers and balance on roller skates.

USING MY HANDS (FINE MOTOR SKILLS)

- Can write in joined-up handwriting.
- Cuts out shapes accurately.
- Produces detailed drawings.
- Ties and unties shoelaces.

LANGUAGE AND COMMUNICATION

- Can now understand 20,000–26,000 words, understands time intervals and seasons of the year, and is aware of mistakes in other people's speech.

At eight to twelve years old
MOVING AROUND (GROSS MOTOR SKILLS)

- Can play games with good coordination and spatial awareness – able to concentrate on strategies in games such as football or netball.

USING MY HANDS (FINE MOTOR SKILLS)

- Can manage more complex activities such as model making, knitting and typing and talk at the same time as less concentration is needed for the control of physical movements.

LANGUAGE AND COMMUNICATION

- Can carry on conversation at a more adult level.

- Follows fairly complex directions with little repetition.

- Has well developed time and number concepts.

How do developmental milestones help us with the identification of possible problems?

Healthy child development is often taken for granted. Parents expect their children to follow a normal developmental path, with at most some slight delays which will even themselves out over time. Parents may start to express concerns if they feel their child is not progressing at the same rate as other children in the family have done or when compared to other children of the same age. Often parents are reassured that their child will catch up in her own time and this is indeed often the case, but some children do have developmental delays which they will not grow out of without support. As children grow, we expect them to learn to read and write, and we take notice of how they are progressing. They grow, develop and learn throughout their lives and we can assess how they are developing through, for example, observing how they play, learn, speak and behave.

Just as the developmental milestones can be used as signposts to a child's 'normal' development, they can also be used to determine whether there is reason to be concerned about a child's progress. There is cause for concern, for example, if a child consistently seems unable to build a tower of six to eight bricks, seems uncomfortable holding a crayon or spoon, or has difficulty with dressing and undressing at an age when she might be expected to be able to do so independently. Individuals vary, for example, in their ability to perform coordinated actions and are more or less clumsy or coordinated in different activities at various times in their lives. Some of these differences in performance appear because of genetic influences, some because of abnormalities in the brain or body acquired during or after birth or because of faulty or incomplete physical experiences.

Max cannot catch balls well and is clumsy in his movements. This makes him frustrated and, as a result, his behaviour reflects this frustration. As Max then kicks out or becomes emotional, he is rejected by other children, which in turn makes him feel even more of a failure. His mother is told that 'there's nothing to worry about...' but she feels that she is at the end of her tether as Max becomes increasingly reluctant to go to school.

Early signs of developmental immaturity

There are a number of early indicators of developmental slowness that may be evident in a child of school age. It is important to note that if some of these signs are present in a younger child, they are not necessarily indicative of developmental immaturity.

- Attention.

- Sitting still.

- Receptive language: a child's understanding of what is said to her.

- Expressive language: how a child expresses herself to others.

- Pencil grip: how she holds her pencil or cutlery.

- Visual skills, such as eye control and difficulties with early reading games and activities.

- Body awareness of themselves and in relation to others.

- The ability to understand and respond to the ways in which other people are expressing themselves through body language.

- Coordination such as catching a ball.

- Immature behaviour including difficulties in taking turns and in controlling her behaviour and impulses.

(Goddard Blythe 2008)

Promoting early development

As parents or teachers you can actively promote a child's development. Make sure you provide plenty of opportunities for outdoor activities and exercise at a level which is appropriate to the child's level of competence and confidence, rather than at the age they *should* be functioning at. Avoid pushing a child through the milestones as if it were a race: it is very important that children have enough time to consolidate skills at one level before they are ready to move on. If a particular milestone then becomes an issue, you will be able to talk with confidence to your health visitor or doctor, based on your observations.

Children do not need expensive electronic toys to have fun; they often tire of them quickly and they do not always live up to the claims made for them. Simple toys and activities encourage children to develop their own creativity and imagination. Use the developmental milestones as sources of inspiration for devising activities which are fun to do and which help develop a child's skills. Look at developing your child's strengths, not just concentrating on what she is struggling to achieve. This is a good way to help her develop awareness of what she is good at!

Make scrap books with photos of your child, drawings, postcards and so on. A personal book which develops over time helps a child to develop many skills including language development, concepts of time, family relationships and so on. Spending time with a child in a calm, supportive environment where good communication can be developed is one of the best gifts you can give her.

Summary

The development of children is influenced by their genetic profile, the quality of their experiences and their learning opportunities. Children develop at different rates and their rate of development may be more advanced in some areas than in others.

Developmental milestones can help professionals identify early on the children who need special attention or additional help in some areas of development when compared to other children. Children with developmental delays may experience additional problems as a result of these delays. For this reason, it is important to intervene early and to seek guidance and support from your health visitor, family doctor and from your child's school. More information follows in the next chapters.

3

Detecting Special Educational Needs

This chapter looks at:

★ what special educational needs are

★ information about dyslexia, dyspraxia and attention deficit hyperactivity disorder

★ symptom checklists for dyslexia, dyspraxia and ADHD

★ an example of a Kids Can Succeed Record Form.

GEMMA'S MOTHER'S CONCERNS

- Is there something wrong with Gemma?
- Will her reading ever improve?
- Has something happened to make her like this?
- Is it my fault she's like this?

What are special educational needs?

Children with special educational needs all have learning difficulties or disabilities that make it harder for them to learn than most children of the same age. These children may need extra or different help from that given to other children of the same age.

Just because a child seems to have special educational needs at one point in time, it doesn't mean he will always be struggling. Schools, parents and programmes can help him to fulfil his potential if difficulties are recognized early enough and the right kind of support is given. Teachers can be trained to provide different types of support, help and activities known as differentiation and many schools will have someone who has a responsibility for coordinating help for children with special educational needs.

Your child's school can provide you with information about the level of support you can expect your child to receive. They can also explain the assessments they have carried out to reach this conclusion.

Early education settings and schools are expected to place great importance on identifying special educational needs as quickly as they can so that help can be given. However, a problem can arise if there is a mismatch between the perceptions of parents and the perceptions of school. You may think there is a problem and they may not. Or even vice-versa.

There are of course many other learning difficulties which may not be recognized or diagnosed, particularly if a child is coping but not doing as well as he might. Schools and families do not always identify children as under-achieving if they appear to be reaching expected goals or are within the average for their class. In the chapters that follow, there are contributions from experts which describe the different ways in which a child's problems may be identified and managed. This process will be infinitely more effective if you as a parent or teacher are well informed and well briefed and can provide these professionals with detailed information and observations. It will also help you to have an understanding of what their roles are.

Use the questionnaires and checklists you will find in the appendices of this book. The more information you can assemble, the better informed you are when making choices and decisions. You may also find that there are some behaviours or difficulties that you have not really noticed before which apply at home, but not in school, or vice-versa. Look back at the developmental milestones to see if these shed any light on your child's problems and also to reflect on whether there might be an issue with primitive and postural reflexes as outlined in Chapter 1 – the symptoms of retained primitive reflexes can be similar to the symptoms of a learning difficulty. For example, if a cluster of primitive reflexes is still present or if postural reflexes are under-developed, they can limit the amount of improvement that is gained from any intervention until the reflex problems have been resolved.

Tips on addressing your concerns

- Ask for information from other people you trust and professionals such as your family doctor or health visitor.

- Speak with your child's teacher and SENCO (special educational needs coordinator) and find out what the school says it can do when concern is expressed.

- Ask the school for copies of any assessments they have carried out with your child and what the implications of these are. Do not accept that your child 'will grow out of it'. Schools have a duty to assess and intervene.

- Speak to your child and see how he feels about himself. Even very young children have insights into how well they are doing compared to their friends.

- Reassure him that he is loved, important, valued and special. Play down incidents of clumsiness, frustration and failure and praise any small positive experience.

- Be kind to yourself: blaming yourself or wondering whether you are at fault in any way and have caused the problem is not as useful as becoming your child's biggest ally and supporter.

Some learning differences you may need to know about

In the following section, you will find information about a number of learning difficulties which are well recognized as causing some children to under-perform and under-achieve in the classroom. Very often there is a degree of overlap (known as comorbidity) which means that a child may be dyslexic as well as dyspraxic for example. If your child has one difficulty, it is reasonably likely that he will have more than one difficulty.

Tips as you find out more

- Keep a file of your information and dated observations. The more information you have that can back up your case, the more likely it is that you will be listened to.

- Always check on the credentials of private or independent specialists. There are professional organizations they should belong to. Advice from your doctor or school may be appropriate here. It is very important that only specialists with recognized qualifications are consulted, as some organizations may be less professional and more commercial in their interests.

Do labels help?

It is well accepted that the sooner a child's difficulties are identified, the better this is for him in the long term both in terms of his learning, but also his confidence, his self-esteem and his attitude towards school and learning. When a child is assessed, the professionals involved in the process are seeking to establish whether the difficulties or patterns of difficulties fit a recognized category or a diagnosis – a label. The diagnosis provides a description of a specific group of symptoms and may indicate what can be done in terms of providing interventions. The diagnosis does not always explain *why* the problem has developed, but focuses on *what* the problem is.

For some parents and teachers, labels are seen as unhelpful because they reduce the child to a list of symptoms which are negative and which can be used to tease and bully children. Children may feel that they can't get any better and that they are stuck with a label which also provides them with an excuse not to try and succeed.

The alternative view is that diagnosis helps children to realize why they are having problems and it provides their parents with an explanation and routes to support. Children who have struggled to achieve and whose self-confidence is low can benefit from programmes which help them to realize that they can and will succeed as many others have before them. A diagnosis can often be a relief if it helps a child to understand that they are not stupid and that their brains are not 'useless'. By collecting evidence, parents and teachers can move forward more readily. Labels can bring much-needed support at many levels, such as extra time in examinations, access to specialist equipment, a recognition of a child's difficulties and, maybe most important, a recognition that the child is not a naughty boy; he is a boy who is struggling to understand why everything seems that much harder for him than for anyone else. He doesn't want to ignore the teacher, but his attention has wandered through no choice of his own. The label provides him with the right to work in conditions which take his difficulties into account and which look for strengths he can develop.

Dyslexia

When completing the following checklist, it is useful to include your child's name, date of birth and the date of completion, so you can use the checklist in meetings with teachers or other professionals at a future date. If a child has several of the indications outlined below, further investigation should be made. The child may be dyslexic, or there may be other reasons that require attention.

Indications of dyslexia[1]

1.   Persisting factors
There are many persisting factors in dyslexia, which can appear from an early age. They will still be noticeable when the dyslexic child leaves school.

These include:

- ☐ Obvious 'good' and 'bad' days, for no apparent reason.
- ☐ Confusion between directional words, e.g. up/down, in/out.
- ☐ Difficulty with sequence, e.g. coloured bead sequence, later with days of the week or numbers.
- ☐ A family history of dyslexia/reading difficulties.

---

[1]   The information in this section is taken from the very useful British Dyslexia Association website (www.bdadyslexia.org.uk) and is printed with their kind permission.

2. Pre-school

- ☐ Has persistent jumbled phrases, e.g. 'cobbler's club' for 'toddler's club'.
- ☐ Use of substitute words, e.g. 'lampshade' for 'lamppost'.
- ☐ Inability to remember the label for known objects, e.g. 'table, chair'.
- ☐ Difficulty learning nursery rhymes and rhyming words, e.g. 'cat, mat, sat'.
- ☐ Later than expected speech development.

Pre-school non-language indicators:

- ☐ May have walked early but did not crawl – was a 'bottom shuffler' or 'tummy wriggler'.
- ☐ Persistent difficulties in getting dressed efficiently and putting shoes on the correct feet.
- ☐ Enjoys being read to but shows no interest in letters or words.
- ☐ Is often accused of not listening or paying attention.
- ☐ Excessive tripping, bumping into things and falling over.
- ☐ Difficulty with catching, kicking or throwing a ball; with hopping and/or skipping.
- ☐ Difficulty with clapping a simple rhythm.

3. Primary-school age

- ☐ Has particular difficulty with reading and spelling.
- ☐ Puts letters and figures the wrong way round.
- ☐ Has difficulty remembering tables, alphabet, formulae, etc.
- ☐ Leaves letters out of words or puts them in the wrong order.
- ☐ Still occasionally confuses 'b' and 'd' and words such as 'no/on'.
- ☐ Still needs to use fingers or marks on paper to make simple calculations.
- ☐ Poor concentration.
- ☐ Has problems understanding what he/she has read.
- ☐ Takes longer than average to do written work.
- ☐ Problems processing language at speed.

Primary-school age non-language indicators:

☐ Has difficulty with tying shoe laces, tie, and dressing.

☐ Has difficulty telling left from right, order of days of the week, months of the year, etc.

☐ Surprises you because in other ways he/she is bright and alert.

☐ Has a poor sense of direction and still confuses left and right.

☐ Lacks confidence and has a poor self image.

What is dyslexia?

The word 'dyslexia' comes from the Greek: *dys-* meaning 'difficulty with', and *lexia* meaning 'words' or 'language'. Dyslexia affects many aspects of learning, not just reading and writing. Dyslexia is not related to intelligence, race or social background. Dyslexia is a learning difficulty that primarily affects the skills involved in accurate and fluent word reading and spelling.

Dyslexia is often thought of as a continuum, ranging from mild to severe, and there are no clear cut-off points. This has caused much disagreement over the years as to whether we can say that dyslexia actually exists as a condition as it can be difficult in some cases to reach a clear diagnosis because there are so many variables. However, when a child is experiencing continued difficulties in learning to read, investigations need to be made. Co-occurring difficulties may be seen in aspects of language, motor coordination, mental calculation, concentration and personal organization, but these are not, by themselves, markers of dyslexia (Rose 2009).

Is dyslexia common?

Figures vary widely regarding the percentage of people who have dyslexia, from 4–5 per cent to up to 10 per cent and above. For example the British Dyslexia Association say that 10 per cent of the British population are dyslexic; 4 per cent severely so. One of the difficulties with being more precise about this is the wide definitions of dyslexia which exist and the wide range of symptoms that can be classified as dyslexic.

When and how would I become aware of dyslexia?

Children are generally born with dyslexia, but it may remain undetected until the child starts school and begins to struggle with aspects of their learning. The link between early language and later reading ability suggests that it is possible to identify dyslexic difficulties from an early age (Snowling, Muter and Carol 2007). The child with dyslexia is often at a disadvantage right from the start in school as his strengths are not in reading, writing spelling and dealing with symbols. Children with dyslexia often do have strengths in other areas such as imagination and creativity and many dyslexic people grow up to be successful in careers such as architecture, engineering and other creative arts. They can also be good at acting, lateral thinking and often make good managers in people-related occupations. If given the appropriate help for their areas of difficulty, there is no reason why a dyslexic person should not be a high achiever and/or gain a university degree – many have done so.

Can both boys and girls have dyslexia?

It used to be thought that more boys than girls were dyslexic but it now appears that boys and girls are almost equally affected, but boys are more likely to identified, perhaps as a result of other associated problem such as poor behaviour and frustration. Recent research suggests that dyslexia is only slightly more common (1.5:1) in boys than girls.[2]

Is dyslexia inherited?

There are a number of theories that suggest different causes for dyslexia and much has been written about this subject. Dyslexia does seem to run in families, although this is not always the case. The International Dyslexia Association states that the causes of dyslexia are 'neurobiological and genetic. Individuals inherit the genetic links for dyslexia. Chances are that one of the child's parents, grandparents, aunts, or uncles is dyslexic' (International Dyslexia Association 2007). There may be other reasons for a child appearing to have some symptoms suggesting dyslexia. This is particularly so in relation to

---

2   Merrill Advanced Study Center, http://merrill.ku.edu.

reading difficulties, where visual difficulties may be the underlying cause. There is more information about this in Chapter 5.

Will it get better or worse? Can dyslexia be cured?

Dyslexia need not be a barrier to success and achievement if it is recognized and if suitable teaching and other strategies are put in place. Teachers can now access training in best practice for dyslexia teaching. This involves teaching which is very structured and multisensory, using as many of the child's senses as possible to support their understanding. There are several ways that teachers and parents can learn more about dyslexia. The British Dyslexia Association and Dyslexia Action (in the UK) offer much information. International references can be found in the 'Useful Resources' section. Universities, colleges and distance learning are also options.

The general consensus is, however, that children with dyslexia can be helped in a number of ways so that they can achieve their potential, but their fundamental learning style will not be changed.

Could anything else be causing the symptoms associated with dyslexia?

It can sometimes be difficult for teachers and parents to decide whether a child has dyslexia or not. Specialist dyslexia teachers have access to a number of tests which can help determine if this is the case. The school SENCO may have additional training in dyslexia and some schools will have dyslexia screening software. However, caution needs to be exercised as these screening tests can sometimes produce results where a child is wrongly classified as at low risk of dyslexia when this is not the case for a number of reasons. A child of average intelligence who has been very well taught in literacy may appear to have few signs of dyslexia on the test, but he will have problems in day-to-day activities in the classroom.

If concerns persist and screening has been inconclusive, then a child may be referred to an educational psychologist for assessment. This can take place through the school, although normally only when the school has exhausted all other appropriate resources. Parents can opt for a private assessment, and there is more information on this in Chapter 7 by Elvie Brown, the educational psychologist. You will also find descriptions of some children and how their difficulties were identified.

Dyslexia-type symptoms can occur when there are eye teaming, eye tracking and perceptual problems that can cause words, letters and numbers to appear to move or jump on a page. Many people mistakenly think that they or their children have dyslexia because they can see 20/20 with or without corrective lenses and still have trouble reversing words, letters and numbers. Many of these same children and adults have never been tested for or told that they may have a vision disorder.[3] There are cases where both problems are present and the child has both dyslexia and visual difficulties. The chapter on vision goes into this in greater depth.

It is also possible that your child does not have dyslexia, but does have literacy difficulties which are not easily labelled. In these cases, further investigation will be needed by the school's special needs coordinator.

Tips for dyslexia friendly classrooms

- Use a multisensory approach to teaching: graphics, diagrams, flowcharts, mind maps, colours, video, and sound.

- Use displays/ flash cards to support key vocabulary and reinforce on a daily basis as a fun, competitive activity.

- Avoid using red and green pens on the whiteboard as this can be hard to read for some children.

- Recognize that whiteboards can be too glaring for some children as can fluorescent light.

- Include problem solving, creative activities, drama: active learning.

- Provide tasks in which students can express creativity in their thinking and reward the thinking, e.g. original comments on material, original interpretation of ideas, ability to reach new conclusions.

---

3   See www.visionandlearning.co.uk.

- Be creative in ways to avoid copying from the board: prepared support sheets/paired work.
- Use coloured dots/different coloured pens if board work cannot be avoided.
- Check that students have understood instructions – ask them to repeat back: provide sequences/stages of the process/activity.
- Wait time: provide at least three seconds of thinking time after a question and after a response.
- Allow individual thinking time, discussion with a partner, then open up for class discussion.
- Make learning an active process with positive feedback and focused praise.
- Recognize and empathize with different learning abilities, but set high expectations, delivered consistently.
- Rehearse orally before writing; ask pupils to talk through what they are going to write.
- Use writing frames to scaffold work. Model it first, be reflective.
- Use cream paper rather than white.
- Avoid too much print on any page: line space at 1.5.
- Give clear time indicators: finish in ten minutes.
- Limit size of paper, use white-boards.
- Make maximum of I.T.

Choose one of the recommended fonts above. Print at least 12 points. Think about colour and coloured paper. Follow the advice in the BDA's Dyslexia Friendly Style Guide.

Dyspraxia

Max, aged nine, is struggling in his class. He does not have effective sensory and filtering systems to enable him to process events going on around him and to ignore sounds in the background. He is thus often in trouble for lacking concentration and not paying attention. His teacher reports that Max has a poor attention span, although he works well on a one to one basis. He is fidgety and over-reacts to events around him. He is clumsy and doesn't always speak clearly. Max says it's not fair that everyone picks on him.

Max's mother is worried that the situation will get worse if steps are not taken to address Max's increasing frustration, anxiety and social isolation. He gets upset and tells her that he has been told off for his poor handwriting and for dropping his books. He is always the last to be chosen as a partner in class activities or team member for sports. Max's teacher is frustrated by his behaviour and has noticed that he frequently asks to go to the toilet as a work avoidance tactic.

What is dyspraxia?

The word 'dyspraxia' also comes from Greek: *dys-* meaning 'difficulty with' and *praxis* which refers to the planning and carrying out of automatic voluntary movements. *Dyspraxia* basically means difficulty getting our bodies to do what we want, when we want and how we want without conscious effort. This disorder relates to the ability to plan and carry out movements so that, for instance, a child's movement skills may be significantly below his performance in other areas. Dyspraxia is a specific developmental disorder which can also involve problems with language, spatial and thought processes. Dyspraxia, developmental coordination disorder (DCD) and perceptual motor dysfunction are all terms used to describe children who may in the past have been labelled unusually clumsy or physically uncoordinated.

Is dyspraxia common?

There is no firm agreement on how many children have dyspraxia, however research suggests that the incidence is about 6 to 10 per cent.[4]

When and how would I become aware of dyspraxia?

By the age of three, many of the symptoms of dyspraxia are often apparent. As a parent, you may be aware that your child managed all the milestones of sitting, crawling and walking, but at a slower rate than might be expected – outside the normal time-frames.

---

4   See www.dyspraxiafoundation.org.uk.

The symptoms of dyspraxia[5]
....

By three years old
Symptoms are evident from an early age. Babies are usually irritable from birth and may exhibit significant feeding problems.

They are slow to achieve expected developmental milestones. For example, by the age of eight months they still may not sit independently.

Many children with dyspraxia fail to go through the crawling stages, preferring to 'bottom shuffle' and then walk. They usually avoid tasks which require good manual dexterity.

Pre-school children – three- to five-year-olds
If dyspraxia is not identified, problems can persist and affect the child's life at school. Increasing frustration and lowering of self-esteem can result.

Children with dyspraxia may demonstrate some of these types of behaviour:

- ☐ Very high levels of motor activity, including feet swinging and tapping when seated, hand-clapping or twisting. Unable to stay still.

- ☐ High levels of excitability, with a loud/shrill voice.

- ☐ May be easily distressed and prone to temper tantrums.

- ☐ May constantly bump into objects and fall over.

- ☐ Hands flap when running.

- ☐ Difficulty with pedalling a tricycle or similar toy.

- ☐ Lack of any sense of danger (jumping from heights, etc.).

- ☐ Continued messy eating and prefer eating with fingers, frequently spill drinks.

- ☐ Avoidance of construction toys, such as jigsaws or building blocks.

- ☐ Difficulty in holding a pencil or using scissors. Drawings may appear immature.

- ☐ Lack of imaginative play. May show little interest in dressing up or in playing appropriately in a home corner.

- ☐ Limited creative play.

---

5   This list of the symptoms of dyspraxia is adapted with the kind permission of the Dyspraxia Foundation in Britain (www.dyspraxiafoundation.org.uk).

- [ ] Isolation within the peer group. Rejected by children of own age and may prefer adult company.
- [ ] They may use either hand for activities: they are not 'right' or 'left' handed.
- [ ] Persistent language difficulties.
- [ ] Sensitive to sensory stimulation: dislike of loud sounds or textures of clothes for example.
- [ ] Limited response to verbal instruction. May be slow to respond and have problems with comprehension.
- [ ] Limited concentration. Tasks are often left unfinished.

By seven years old
Problems may include:

- [ ] Difficulties in adapting to a structured school routine.
- [ ] Difficulties in Physical Education lessons.
- [ ] Slow at dressing. Unable to tie shoe laces.
- [ ] Barely legible handwriting.
- [ ] Immature drawing and copying skills.
- [ ] Limited concentration and poor listening skills.
- [ ] Literal use of language.
- [ ] Inability to remember more than two or three instructions at once.
- [ ] Slow completion of class work.
- [ ] Continued high levels of motor activity.
- [ ] Hand flapping or clapping when excited.
- [ ] Tendency to become easily distressed and emotional.
- [ ] Problems with coordinating a knife and fork.
- [ ] Inability to form relationships with other children.
- [ ] Sleeping difficulties, including wakefulness at night and nightmares.
- [ ] Reporting of physical symptoms, such as migraine, headaches, feeling sick.

Can both boys and girls have dyspraxia?

Dyspraxia appears to be three to four times more common in boys than girls – boys are four times more likely to be referred for assessment.

Is dyspraxia inherited?

According to the Dyspraxia Foundation, many parents of children who have dyspraxia can identify another member of the family with similar difficulties: as dyspraxia is more often found in boys than girls this may be a father, grandfather, uncle or cousin. Sometimes, during the course of an assessment fathers realize that they experienced similar difficulties as a child.

Will it get better? Can dyspraxia be cured?

Dyspraxia can affect children mildly or to a much more significant degree, in that it interferes with successful living and learning. With early identification, recognition and support, children and adults can learn strategies to help them with their difficulties. As dyspraxia can occur in children with normal or above normal intelligence, children may develop a sense of failure and frustration and under-achieve unless they are supported. In this respect, their disability is even more frustrating as they fail to reach their potential. There are several professionals who could be involved in the diagnosis of dyspraxia as it often overlaps with other conditions such as ADHD, Asperger's syndrome and dyslexia and therefore the symptoms to be observed and investigated are multi-faceted.

When the classroom is adapted to reduce distracting stimuli and direct strategies are implemented uniformly by teachers and other adults working with children, the outcome is likely to be far more positive for all concerned. If teachers become more aware of sensory regulation issues, and provide sensory regulating equipment, such as stress balls, children with dyspraxia will be in a better position to cope with the demands being made on their senses all day long.

Could anything else be causing the behaviour and symptoms associated with dyspraxia?

There are a number of professionals who may be involved in finding out whether a child does have dyspraxia. The first step again is to speak to your child's teacher and see if there is a problem in the classroom, in the playground or in physical activities. This information will be useful when you speak with a health professional such as your family doctor or the health visitor. The professionals who can support and advise you on whether your child has dyspraxia, or whether there is some other reason for their difficulties include:

- speech and language therapists

- occupational therapists

- paediatricians (doctors who provide specialist medical care to infants, children and adolescents)

- physiotherapists

- educational psychologists.

The process of assessment will vary and waiting time will also vary.

Tips for helping children who are having difficulties with fine motor skills

Difficulty	Strategies
Handwriting difficulties	Practice multisensory letter formation, e.g. sandpaper letters, sky writing, rice trays Use pencil grips, writing lines, stencils
Difficulties with dressing and fastening clothes Difficulty with using tools, utensils and cutlery	Suggest loose-fit easy on/easy off clothing and Velcro fastenings Break down each task into small sections to be mastered one-by-one

Difficulty walking in straight line, bumps into people and things Difficulties running, hopping, jumping, catching or kicking balls	Provide balance or wobble boards, walking on the line and hand to hand throwing using bean bags or water-filled balloons
Reacts to all stimuli without discrimination Attention span is poor Distracted in open-plan environments Flits between activities Disturbs others	Allow child to choose activities which meet child's own interests Avoid disturbing child when on task Avoid fluorescent lights, fluttering ceiling displays Keep wall displays to a minimum Promote a 'no-disturbance' culture showing respect for each child's work space
Unable to remember and/or follow instructions	Get the attention of the child before giving instructions Use simple language with visual prompts Provide time to process the information. Use activities, demonstrations and pictures

These tips are adapted from information on the Dyspraxia Foundation website.

Attention deficit hyperactivity disorder
What is ADHD?

The three primary characteristics of attention deficit hyperactivity disorder (ADHD) are inattention, hyperactivity and impulsivity. The signs and symptoms a child with ADHD has depends on which characteristics predominate. Children with ADHD may be:

- inattentive, hyperactive and impulsive (the most common form of ADHD)

- hyperactive and impulsive, but able to pay attention

- inattentive, but not hyperactive or impulsive.

Which one of these children may have ADD/ADHD?

'Callum is on the go all the time: he just never stops. He wears me out. He's always blurting out stupid things and doing things without thinking. His teacher says he's got no concentration at all. He has so much trouble paying attention, it drives everyone crazy.'

'Sara is so dreamy: she's missing so much in lessons and getting behind. She should be doing a lot better than she is, but she's just so forgetful...'

The answer is possibly both of them!

Is ADHD common?

The estimate is that among school-aged children between 3 and 5 per cent will have a diagnosis of ADHD with some evidence for higher levels in areas of socio-economic disadvantage. ADHD is usually first diagnosed in childhood and often lasts into adulthood.

When and how would I become aware of ADHD?

Most children, at one time or another, have difficulty with concentration, focus and behaving in the right way for the situation they are in. With children who have ADHD, the symptoms persist and learning becomes very difficult. Children who have problems in school but not at home or socially are not generally considered to have ADHD. Equally, a child who is hyperactive or inattentive only at home but whose schoolwork and social relationships with other children are not affected by their behaviour is not likely to be diagnosed with ADHD.

Children usually start showing symptoms by the time they start school. Some very impulsive children are diagnosed as early as two or three years old whereas others tend to develop more severe symptoms around the age of nine or ten. These children may have always had ADHD but were able to compensate for the condition. As they get older and school requires more work and more organizational skills, these children may reach a point where they become unable to compensate and exhibit 'full blown' ADHD symptoms. Some children may remain undiagnosed until they are in their teens. More recently adults have been diagnosed as having the condition – they had the disorder as children but were not properly identified until adulthood.

Symptoms and signs of ADHD[6]

A child with ADHD might:

- struggle to maintain attention and/or daydream a lot

- appear not to listen

- be easily distracted from schoolwork or play

- be forgetful

- be in a state of constant motion, unable to stay seated

- squirm and fidget

- be overly talkative

- be unable to play quietly

- act and speak without thinking

- have trouble taking turns

- interrupt others.

Can both boys and girls have ADHD?

The male-to-female ratio ranges from 4:1 for the predominantly hyperactive impulsive type to 2:1 for the predominantly inattentive subtype.

Is ADHD inherited?

ADHD does tend to run in families. However, there may be a number of other causes that can contribute to a diagnosis of ADHD, such as visual factors, which are described in Chapter 5. In addition, for example, a lack of natural play in early childhood has been cited as

---

6   Adapted from www.cdc.gov/ncbddd/adhd/facts.html.

one possible cause of ADHD, as scientists have come to the conclusion that unstructured play is vital to the development of young minds (Panskepp 2007).

Will it get better? Can ADHD be cured?

ADHD often continues into adulthood. According to some sources, many children simply outgrow ADHD. About half of those affected appear to function normally by young adulthood, but a significant number will have problems that persist into adult life. According to the Mental Health Foundation, approximately two out of five children with ADHD continue to have difficulties at age 18 (Mental Health Foundation 2000). These may take the form of depression, irritability, anti-social behaviour and attention problems.

Could anything else be causing the behaviour and symptoms associated with ADHD?

Anxiety, depression and certain types of learning disabilities can have similar symptoms to ADHD. Many children with ADHD will have other developmental difficulties, particularly with motor coordination and learning. Hearing problems such as deafness or glue ear can make it hard for a child to follow instructions and make them appear inattentive.

Prolonged periods of insufficient sleep may cause poor concentration, distractibility or dreaminess. This may be the case if home circumstances are preventing good sleep or if the child has a condition known as *sleep apnoea*. Sleep apnoea is usually a chronic (ongoing) condition that disrupts your child's sleep three or more nights each week. Those affected often move out of deep sleep and into light sleep with breathing pausing or becoming shallow. This results in poor sleep quality that makes your child tired during the day. Sleep apnoea is one of the leading causes of excessive daytime sleepiness. The most common cause of sleep apnoea in children is enlarged tonsils. Nowadays sleep apnoea is a common reason for recommending that a young child has their tonsils out.

Many children are very active or easily distracted or have difficulty concentrating. If these behaviours are relatively mild, they should not be considered a disorder. ADHD requires a medical diagnosis by a doctor, usually a child or adolescent psychiatrist, a paediatrician or paediatric neurologist or a family doctor. Other professionals such as psychologists, speech therapists, teachers and health visitors may also be involved in the assessment of a child with possible ADHD. There is no single diagnostic test for ADHD so different sorts of information needs to be gathered. To be diagnosed with ADHD, a child must have symptoms which have started before the age of seven, and which make his life considerably more difficult both socially and academically.

Summary

When your child is failing and you are at your wit's end, it helps to have a plan. Please read, highlight, tick, cross and make notes on the checklists and advice in this chapter. Then refer back to the tips on page 44. Maintain a good relationship with your child's school by being clear about what you expect and why. The information included here is for guidance only and cannot be used to provide evidence of a diagnosis.

The following record form can be used by parents to gather the evidence about their child and to help them to organize the information they are given. It helps by working logically through a system of working out what the child's problems might be and what actions can be taken.

Example of Kids Can Succeed Record Form
Pupil's name: Gemma Chater
Date of birth: 11/06/2001
Person completing this form and relationship to child: Kim Chater (mother)
Date record started: September 2009

Section one

Ask people who know the child well what the child's strengths and areas of concern are. Ask the child as well if appropriate.

Strengths	Areas of concern
Hard working and wants to please. Very sociable. Very good vocabulary.	A bit clumsy. Not able to remember her spellings and doesn't like reading. School says her memory is weak.

Section two

Use the checklists by ticking, highlighting and making notes. Attach copies and summarize below.

Checklists used (Include dates)	Comments
Dyslexia Dyspraxia INPP	I have filled out the checklists and Gemma has completed all the Screen Learning games. I think these do show that Gemma does have a problem and it's not just her memory.

Section three

Use this section to summarize any reports, meetings and information from health professionals.

Professional (include dates)	Comments
Health visitor (September 2009)	No early problems.
Doctor (September 2009)	Doctor says Gemma's hearing is OK, but she does often have ear infections and colds.
Hearing (September 2009)	See above. I have asked for Gemma to be further investigated because I don't think she hears as well as she should.
Eyesight (March 2008)	Gemma doesn't wear glasses. She had an eye test last year.

Section four
Other information.

I think the forms say it all really. There are enough signs there to say that Gemma has a real problem which she needs help with. I asked Gemma what she thought and she wants to get better at her reading and spelling.

Section five
Details of subsequent discussions with school/others.

Date and people present	Notes and action points: what will happen next and by what date?
16 October 2009 Kim Chater Mr Salmon (class teacher)	We looked at Gemma's books and her reading record. I gave them a copy of her Screen Learning printout and the checklists I had filled in. Mr Salmon has made an appointment for Gemma to see the special needs teacher.
13 November 2009 Kim Chater Mr Salmon (class teacher) Miss Skuse (special needs teacher)	I talked about how Gemma is starting to feel a real failure and won't read with me at home. Mr Salmon mostly listened to what Miss Skuse had to say. Miss Skuse agreed that Gemma did seem to have difficulties which may be dyslexia and/or dyspraxia. She agreed to work with Mr Salmon to carry out some assessments. A date was set for 17 November to review progress and talk about the tests carried out.

Part II:

Interventions for Home and School

4

Movement and Learning

This chapter looks at:

★ why children may be underperforming at school

★ a neurodevelopmental approach to learning difficulties

★ balance

★ movement programmes

★ handwriting

★ the importance of good self-esteem.

Dealing with children who are lazy, can't concentrate or are not ready to learn: the importance of early intervention

Teachers have many demands on their time and they are often working with large numbers of pupils with a dizzying breadth of needs. They may have limited access to specialized professionals such as speech and language therapists, occupational therapists or educational psychologists. Scarce resources mean that a child who is not perceived to be a concern is less likely to be referred for assessment.

Children start school at different stages depending on, for example, which country they live in. Whatever age a child starts school, some will not be developmentally ready, as any early years professional will know. Many children entering school haven't yet developed the skills they need for learning. There is growing concern, for example, about the speech, language and communication skills of those children who are not yet ready, and this has been recognized by the British government in new initiatives to support teachers in identifying these needs.

Research indicates that early detection and intervention are key to altering 'developmental learning trajectories' for children, with consequent benefits such as more efficient later learning and enabling the complexity of learning to increase.

Quite small inefficiencies in the sensory processing systems that provide information to the brain during learning are now associated with major effects on learning trajectories. These subtle impairments, when combined with unsupportive environments can lead to long-term difficulties in terms of well-being and success (Goswami 2008). In order to learn efficiently, children's sensory systems must develop normally alongside their development of emotional processing: for example the way that the child is feeling about their learning. Developmental psychology shows that a child's self-esteem, sense of identity and 'inner working model' of her value as a person who is deserving of love and support from others depends on responsive care-giving and security of attachment, and good quality social relationships.

Whether a child qualifies for support can be envisioned using the analogy of height: whether a child is small or not depends on how small (or delayed) she is compared to other children of her age. If she is small, but not quite small enough, she won't necessarily be seen as needing support even though she has significant needs. So children who are just tall enough not to cause concern may be ignored when resources are limited and there are 'shorter' children whose needs have to be addressed first.

Going without a diagnosis: three years old on the inside and ten years old on the outside

Currently identification of dyslexia does not take place until a child reaches the age of eight or nine (Goswami 2008). By this age, a child's ability to learn effectively may already have been undermined. There are other children though, who may not be spotted early on in their schooling because they have good or at least average underlying ability. As the demands of the curriculum increase, however, their strategies to cope begin to break down and their performance begins to dip. They struggle to maintain their focus or their eyes cause reading problems, or they can't follow instructions and complete independent activities. It is as if they are a three-year-old on the inside and a ten-year-old on the outside. They have learned enough strategies to seem as if they are coping but are emotionally and developmentally operating at a much younger level – they have used their intelligence to observe and copy what other children are doing. These children avoid circumstances they know they can't cope with and sometimes they lash out with tantrums and behaviours associated with much younger children. These children are often able to compensate for their underlying problems to produce work which is 'good enough', but which does not truly reflect what they are capable of. At this point they may be identified by their teachers as lazy, unfocused or making little effort and daydreaming.

When these children grow up disappointing themselves and the adults who care about them, the long-term effects can be catastrophic. The children feel inadequate in terms of the results they achieve and when they compare themselves with other children in their class or group. They are often acutely aware that they *could* improve and don't know why they can't.

MAX'S STORY

Max, aged ten, was struggling at primary school and was referred to me for neurodevelopmental delay assessment by an educational psychologist because of his early developmental history and his learning difficulties. Following a full neurodevelopmental delay assessment, he worked on a movement-based programme we developed which led to significant improvements. Max worked on a developmental movement programme devised by the Institute for Neuro-Physiological Psychology (INPP). He followed one of the reflex inhibition and stimulation programmes which INPP practitioners will use, once there has been a thorough evaluation of the child's profile and a detailed discussion with parents. An initial screening form indicates whether this approach may be appropriate for a particular child. He is now coping successfully at his secondary school after a shaky start when his underlying abilities and difficulties were not fully understood.

Max's mother

'As a mother you have got to judge and make many decisions after one's simple gut feeling and motherly instinct. From a very young age onwards (probably already at nursery when he was about three) I was never quite sure about Max's progress and probably also his independence (like dressing himself, etc.) in comparison to his peers. The other issue with him was always a tendency to clumsiness, being uncoordinated (which affects sports but also just lots of easy general tasks, like dropping things a lot, bumping into things, etc.) and being quite fidgety, as well as sometimes very lacking in concentration. The result of all these various issues was that it also affected his confidence...

After endless talks with friends, family and especially teachers who were always very optimistic about Max and tried to console us with "they all get there in their own time" we decided to have him properly tested (when Max was nine) by an independent educational psychologist. As a mother you just know your child, and I knew that time would not cure him. Our suspicions were confirmed – Max was diagnosed as a child with a classic dyslexic profile, probably also some dyspraxic elements. The suggestion was to get a specialist dyslexia teacher and that he would benefit from exercises to address his primary reflexes which should have developed back when a baby/toddler, helping his coordination, helping him fight clumsiness, but also with his concentration, writing and reading. We followed this programme for about one year and persevered with the exercises. It helped Max with his writing and definitely improved his awareness of his surroundings. Max had a really good year last year at school – everything seemed to start falling into place and one could see it clearly on his results at the end of the year!

The programme needs perseverance and I admit, although they are only five minutes a day, it was still an extra task for myself and Max at the end of our generally always busy days...but then it also gave Max the prospect of help with his issues, which clearly bothered him too, and stopped him from achieving how he would like to have done. He so much wanted to do well, so therefore he also understood that it is important to do his exercises, because there was a very good reason for them. It was probably also a good exercise to help him getting more focused.'

Max's comments

'Some bits of the programme I enjoyed more and some less, but it was definitely worth it. I think I am less fidgety and I am now much better, but it also helped me in my English and reading.'

Conclusion

Max is one of the lucky ones. His parents were able and willing to take him to someone who was not only able to assess his abilities, but who understood that sometimes children need a different approach if they are to achieve long-term success.

Moving to learn: a neurodevelopmental approach to learning difficulties

There is a growing body of evidence to support the long-held theory that control of balance, motor skills and integration of early reflexes *are* linked to academic achievement. Now, not only can these problems be identified by teachers within the school system, but a series of studies carried out in schools in the United Kingdom since 2000 has shown that, in many cases, something can be done about them. (Goddard Blythe 2005)

What role does movement play in specific learning difficulties?

- *Dyslexia*: problems in the direction and sequencing of movement.

- *Dyspraxia*: difficulties with the visualization, imitation and organization of motor output.

- *Attention deficit hyperactivity disorder (ADHD)*: difficulty with the inhibition of movement.

- *Autistic spectrum disorders*: lack of perceptual coherence, resulting in part from poor sensory motor integration.

(Goddard Blythe 2005)

Who is using movement programmes and why should I?

Around the world, teachers, occupational therapists, physiotherapists and other professionals are learning more about the relationship between early development, physical development and effective learning in the classroom. Armed with this knowledge, they are empowered as they apply their understanding and observe the results.

An Australian educator and pioneer in the field of developmental movement programmes and other approaches to learning difficulties, Barbara Pheloung, who I had the honour of working with at a school in Fiji, has devised the 'Move to Learn' programme. These movement sequences develop natural integration and learning readiness through carrying out a series of developmental movements on a daily basis. The sequences mimic early human movement development and help to integrate the most commonly retained primitive reflexes and underdeveloped postural reflexes. Barbara has also written extensively about learning difficulties. Her work is based on her many years' experience working with children as well as her own daughter's struggles in learning.[1]

The following is adapted from one of Barbara Pheloung's publications and relates to how she would like to see teachers and professionals reach agreement on some key issues.

Think about whether you would you agree with all/some of the statements below:

- *All children want to learn, or wanted to learn at some point in their education.* This point underlines the importance of early intervention rather than waiting for children to fail to 'catch up'. By working together as a team and establishing a close partnership with parents, perspectives of performance at home and school can complement one another and lead to a more coherent approach towards preventing failure.

- *New research is finding that the brain can be changed. If one part is injured, then other parts may take over the same function.* Norman Doidge's book *The Brain That Changes Itself* (2007) describes

---

1   Barbara Pheloung's DVD and books are available at www.movetolearn.com.au.

how the brain has the ability to adapt and change and he provides a guide to current research in neuroscience.

- *Movement and learning go together. You can't learn without movement.* Our eyes must work together efficiently for many functions, our ears and noses have parts which move constantly and our whole body adjusts constantly as we absorb information.

- *About 20 per cent of all people in the western world have to struggle academically and don't reach their potential.* The figure of 20 per cent is well known. However the reason why people struggle may be due to many different factors, and not everyone can achieve their potential regardless of support. It is important to accept that not all problems can be solved and that there are times when no one can reach a conclusion about the specific reasons for a child's difficulties.

- *There is a universal pattern in the way humans develop as babies and toddlers. Those who don't follow the stages and order of this sequence may go on to struggle academically.* This is covered in Chapter 2 where the 'normal' developmental milestones are described in detail.

- *It is not so important when a child goes through these developmental stages as that a child goes through these stages in the correct order and for sufficient length of time.* Developmental programmes such as Barbara's Move to Learn programme and the INPP programme work on this principle. What distinguishes them from other programmes is the practice of going right back to the very beginning of movement training, using natural movements in a developmental sequence. This can lead to improved coordination, balance and, it is proposed, educational performance. These programmes are outlined later in this chapter.

- *Each person with learning difficulties has different needs and abilities.* It is the task of professionals, in partnership with parents, to identify and make the best of a child's abilities as well as her needs. By using the symptom checklists and the record form, you can chart a child's strengths and difficulties.

- *Humans are resourceful and if they find it hard to do something, they will usually find a way round it that is easier for them. This can sometimes be at a cost however, as they will be constantly compensating.* Think of something you found hard to learn such as driving; what strategies did you use to cope with the mental, physical and emotional aspects of this? Is there maybe a better way you could have done this?

- *We need to address the cause, not the symptoms.* If anything, this is the message of this book: we have to address why a child is not achieving to the levels she should. If schools only look at spelling problems, reading problems, maths problems and emotional and behaviour problems without looking at the causes, time is being wasted and the focus is in the wrong place. If teachers and parents know where to look for the causes, they are more likely to achieve successful results.

(Pheloung 2004)

The ABC of Learning

Goddard Blythe has written extensively on the importance of skills which support learning. The 'ABC of Learning' is a way of understanding what children need as the foundation of their learning (Goddard Blythe 2009).

A = Attention

B = Balance

C = Coordination

In her book, *Attention, Balance and Coordination: The ABC of Learning Success* (2009), Goddard Blythe stresses the importance of the relationship between these three elements in terms of the child's readiness to learn. If a child cannot maintain good control over her body, she is not well-equipped for learning.

Children who are not achieving may have reading, writing or behavioural problems. Instead of helping them only by practising these skills, we need to address the causes of the problems such as poorly organized movement patterns. Once a child has achieved these movement skills to age appropriate levels, she is then perceived to be ready to learn. Children do mature at different rates and these individual differences can mean that within a class, there are children who are of the right age physically, but developmentally they are lagging behind others born at the same time and need more time involved in general physical activities. Teachers can learn to identify whether children are ready for formal learning as balance, posture and motor skills (how children move) can provide indications of how mature their nervous system is. While all three elements, attention, balance and coordination, are important, in the next section balance is focused on because balance underpins the ability to pay attention and the ways in which the body is able to coordinate movements effectively.

Why balance is important

Balance is fundamentally important in so many aspects of our lives and yet many children are not developing good balance and coordination. Good balance is achieved with a minimum amount of energy and good postural control. Sometimes we balance when not moving (static balance) and sometimes when moving (dynamic balance). Although we are generally unaware of it, the body is continually making changes to posture in response to the information that is received from our sensory systems. To control our posture to sit, stand or maintain any other position we have to continually adapt how we move according to the information we are receiving from our senses. Vision is just one of the senses which tells us how our bodies are positioned in relation to our surroundings.

The visual system cannot be used until birth, and develops rapidly in the first weeks of life. The foundations for the eye–hand skills necessary for learning in the classroom later on are linked to the balance mechanism and to motor development in the first months of life. Many children can compensate for poor balance as long as they are able to use their eyes to tell them where they are in space, but this can overload the visual system. This can then cause visual stress and difficulty processing visual information in a busy environment. The

75

balance mechanism should support the visual system by providing it with accurate information about the child's position in space, and the child who has to use her vision as a compensatory system will find it very difficult to give full attention to finer visual tasks.

Feedback from the body relays information about how our limbs and body are positioned in relation to one another. The *vestibular system* provides information about head position and movement. Children may appear to be well balanced and coordinated, yet when they are asked to carry out a one-legged balance, they are often unable to do so.

There are a number of signs you might observe:

- swaying from side to side or forwards and backwards
- flapping or waving arms out to the side to help achieve balance
- fixating: staring at one point fixedly
- tongue sticking out or facial grimaces.

A simple test of balance

Children need good enough balance to be able to stand on one leg, walk across uneven surfaces and use PE equipment safely in school. We all use inbuilt reflexes that allow subtle changes in balance. When we are pushed for example, or when we trip on an uneven pavement slab, we automatically outstretch our arms to save ourselves. Children with neurological immaturity do not always have the appropriate reflex working effectively. They often compensate for poor balance by 'fixing' at the head and neck, or by holding their arms closely to their side to try to maintain some stability.

The simple test below can be carried out with groups of children and the results recorded using the signs above. You may want to note which leg the child chooses to balance on and then compare that by asking her to change leg and try again.

Is the child's preferred leg the same as her preferred writing hand? This would be the most efficient form of body organization. When we are right handed, ideally we should be right eye, ear and leg dominant as well.

Instructions

The child should first stand with her feet together (bare feet) with her hands at her sides. Ask the child to bend one knee, keeping her knees together. A child should be able to stand on one leg, with her eyes open, for the following lengths of time according to her age:

- three and a half to four years: 8 seconds

- six years: 10 seconds on right or left leg

- eight years: 30 seconds on right or left leg.

Significance of test outcomes

If a child has difficulties with balance, it is possible that she will experience difficulties with sitting in the classroom and she may tire quickly and slump in her seat. A child with poor postural stability will find it difficult to maintain a good posture in class. This in turn may affect looking, listening, copying from a board and the ability to use arms and hands efficiently.

Supporting the development of balance at home and in the classroom

There are some simple strategies which can help a child who has difficulties with balance which can be used at home and school:

- Build in rest times.

- Try a sloped surface for writing.

- Don't insist on the upright posture: if a child needs to sit with one foot tucked under her and the other leg extended in order to stabilize her body, allow her to do so.

- If she needs to support her head to write, allow her to do so if working for long periods. She can either write or sit up straight, but not necessarily both!

- Look at introducing a class-based movement programme such as Move to Learn, or use your imagination to create a simple circuit of exercises that include balance, coordination and stamina building.

The benefits of physical exercise

Exercise optimizes the brain and the whole person for learning. It creates the right environment for all our 100 billion nerve cells according to Dr John Ratey, a professor of psychiatry at Harvard Medical School and the co-author of *Spark*, a book about how our brains change when we exercise (2008). He puts forward the case that exercise improves attention, motivation, executive function skills and decreases anxiety. At the Learning and the Brain Conference in 2007, he presented information about how even moderate exercise could 'supercharge' mental circuits to sharpen thinking.

Ratey found that children expressed views that exercising before class and moving during class made schoolwork seem easier. What he found ironic is that some schools have cut back on PE in favour of academic subjects when actually research is showing that physical exercise is exactly what children need to excel academically.

Exercises everyone can benefit from

Box press ups on all fours with hands flat. Bend the arms and lower head towards the floor. Return to starting position. Repeat five times without 'snapping' elbows.

Wall press ups facing the wall with feet shoulder width apart. Place flat hands on the wall at shoulder level. Slowly bend elbows and move head towards wall. Repeat five times.

When a movement programme is called for

For some children the strategies and exercises above may not be sufficient because they do not address their level of developmental need. If there are primitive and postural reflex problems which are affecting children's ability to function to their best potential, the strategies above may not work effectively because they are targeted at too high a level in terms of brain development. These children may need to go back to a more basic level of intervention so that their true intelligence can operate more effectively.

Developmental movement programmes have been shown to lead to gains and improvements in the following:

- maturation of physical skills

- coordination

- classroom behaviours

- reading and drawing

- concentration

- self-confidence.

For such children, you may want to consider looking into using either the school-based programme developed by the Institute for Neuro-Physiological Psychology in Chester in the UK or the Move to Learn programme developed by teachers and occupational therapists in Australia. Both of these organizations have websites with very comprehensive information and checklists to help you to learn more about whether a developmental movement programme is appropriate for your child. For further details please see the 'Useful Resources' in Appendix IV.

The INPP programme

Devised by the Institute for Neuro-Physiological Psychology, the INPP school programme is based on a clinical programme that has been used since the 1970s. It is designed to 'tackle the basis of the learning pyramid and to give the child a solid foundation on which to build his other learning experiences'. The exercises are aimed primarily at children with coordination difficulties, and with children experiencing reading, writing and copying problems. They can also be used in general physical education lessons.

The programme was recognized as one of their 'Inspiring Partnerships' by the Youth Sports Trust.[2] A DVD of the programme in action would form a useful resource for any school wanting to adopt this approach. The school found that children who followed the programme showed improvement in fine and gross motor skills, muscular strength

---

2   www.youthsporttrust.org.

and endurance, balance and spatial awareness. They also improved in terms of body image, confidence and self-esteem. Children who were previously very restless and lacked concentration developed enough muscular endurance to be able to sit for longer and strength and agility to sustain handwriting for longer. It is interesting to note that 75 per cent of the children in the original project made an average gain of five standardized scores on reading (NFER) and the same number made over 24 months progress in reading age, while others gained at least 16 months. (This information comes from the booklet which accompanies the DVD.)

A teacher does need to be trained by the Institute to carry out these exercises and there is information on the website.

> The programme centres on a series of developmental movements that are carried out each day under teachers' supervision. These are based on movements normally made by the developing child in the first year of life.
>
> All exercises are carried out on the floor and help to develop proper head alignment with the body (the basis for good posture), the ability to use left and right sides, and upper and lower sections of the body in different ways (the basis for coordination). Only when a child can complete these very simple movements with automaticity does he/she move on to repeat the movements in a more challenging position. By using **natural movements** in a development sequence, improved coordination becomes an integrated function, rather than a skill, which has only been learned as a result of practice. (INPP 2009)

The Move to Learn programme

This Australian programme equally centres on a series of developmental movements that are carried out each day under teachers' supervision. It uses a simple programme which is in use in many countries where access to more sophisticated programmes and interventions are not available. Currently there are research programmes related to this being carried out in Australia and Poland and it is extensively used for training in countries such as South Africa.

Internationally, there are a number of developmental movement-based programmes that are in use in pre-school settings, schools and specialist clinics. It is important that the programmes are appropriate to the child's level of development and needs, and that those running them have a clear understanding of these needs:

> Sensory systems not only form foundations for mastery, security and physical, emotional and social interactions but also contribute to important perceptions of experience that help more abstract thinking and perception. In doing so they establish stronger lower brain processing to serve higher processing for language and classroom learning. (Steer, cited in Pheloung 2006, p.36)

In the next section, links are made between posture, sensory issues and issues relating to handwriting.

Handwriting

There is considerable variation in the age at which children are developmentally ready to read and write. It is generally accepted that boys are often later than girls in developing the skills they need for reading and writing such as the ability to sit still and to have the hand and finger control needed to hold a pencil comfortably (fine motor skills). They are also often later than girls in developing their language skills. Handwriting is influenced by the development of sensorimotor skills: how the brain interprets sensations it is receiving from, for example, the eyes, ears, skin, and how it organizes physical responses such as gripping the pencil with appropriate force and being able to control the appearance, legibility and fluency of the script.

Handwriting is a high-level executive skill, and problems with it can sometimes be an indicator of an underlying developmental immaturity. If the child is under six years of age they may not be ready physiologically for formal schooling, even though they are within the average range regarding their overall development. Challenges can be easily missed and misunderstood when an intelligent child is performing within this average range, but not to the level they are capable of. When you observe a child writing or engaged in any other desk-based activity, there are many factors which can affect the quality of the child's experience and achievement. Whatever the child's age, check for 'obvious' factors that may be affecting handwriting:

- *Posture:* How is the child sitting? Are her legs wrapped around the chair? Is she holding her head? Is her tongue sticking out?

- *Sensory issues:* Is she fidgeting and distracted, struggling to sit still and pay attention?

- Is she struggling to maintain focus on instructions, and is she unable to ignore what is going on around her?

WHAT'S GOING ON WHEN CARA IS WRITING?

Cara is nine. She is verbally bright and responds well when the subject interests her. She doesn't write very well: her writing is a bit untidy, it slopes across the page and is badly spaced and organized. She holds her pen awkwardly. She flops over the desk and doesn't seem to hear your instructions. She hates school and drives her parents crazy at home.

What if Cara is struggling as she writes because her developmental profile means that it is difficult for her to:

Drawing reprinted with permission from *Miracle Children* by Anna R. Buck © 2008

- sit on her chair without wrapping her legs around the chair legs to stabilize her upper body

- sit upright because it makes her so tired to maintain this position

- write neatly straight down the page because she doesn't know she isn't doing this

- keep the paper and pen under control because she's propping up her head.

Activity

Imagine if you were to observe Cara in your class: What do you see? How many sensory activities are going on as she tries to complete a writing activity? Look around your class and make a note of how many of the children are:

- propping up their heads

- wrapping their feet around the chair

- sticking out their tongue as they concentrate

- slouching

- holding their pencil awkwardly

- being distracted by sounds around them

- producing writing which slopes across the page.

(Adapted from Cheatum and Hammond 2000)

Drawing reprinted with permission from *Miracle Children* by Anna R. Buck © 2008

There are many reasons why Cara and other children may be experiencing these problems and a developmental programme will not be a miracle cure; however, as a class-based intervention which takes a minimal amount of time on a daily basis, it is well worth considering.

Occupational therapists recognize that a common reason why children hold their pencil incorrectly relates to children being expected to participate in writing activities before their hands are developmentally ready. Children need to have strong flexible muscles in their hands and fingers before they can comfortably manipulate a pencil.

Activities to improve pre-writing skills

Some games and activities which help with pre-writing skills include:

- bead threading patterns

- moulding playdough

- squeezing sponges

- using a bucket of water, 'paint' letters on the ground with a paint brush

- posting pennies into a piggy bank

- wheelbarrow walking on hands

- finger rhymes (for examples see Appendix II).

There are many good ideas in Tracey Beckerleg's book, *Fun with Messy Play* (2009).

The implications of difficulties with handwriting: can't write neatly, must try harder...

When pupils can write fluently, the process does not interfere with other mental processes. If writing is a challenge, a child has to use more mental energy to carry out a given task, leaving her with less capacity for generating ideas, selecting vocabulary and planning what she wants to write. Writing is hard to hide and, as a result, children who have difficulty with it will often feel very vulnerable in school. They become conscious of the effort they have to make to produce work which is often criticized. They notice other children writing faster and more neatly than they can and, if their writing is terrible, then somehow this means they are not trying, have a poor attitude or are not able to express themselves. However, ignoring poor handwriting fails to address a significant and continuing obstacle to pupils' achievement. Bad handwriting isn't just hard to read – it can limit exam success by as much as 40 per cent.

> When pupils can write fluently, the process does not interfere with other mental processes. If they struggle, they have to use more mental and physical energy to complete the task. This leaves less energy and mental capacity for generating ideas, selecting vocabulary and mental recall. (Medwell, Strand and Wray 2008)

So ignoring poor handwriting fails to address a significant and continuing obstacle to pupil achievement and it needs to be treated with sensitivity, based on a sound understanding on underlying factors that may be influencing performance.

Handwriting can also be a physical strain.

When a child produces untidy letter formation which does not sit on the line, the pressure she exerts often causes her hand and arm to tire easily, so she avoids writing whenever she can. She is not consciously aware of why her hand, wrist, arm, shoulder and neck ache as this is what every day is like in school now that she is expected to write.

A child with a dyspraxic profile may produce untidy letter formation which does not sit on the line. The pressure she exerts will often cause her hand and arm to tire easily, leading to reluctance to write. Children may not consciously be aware of discomfort in their hand, wrist, arm, shoulder and neck if this is their daily experience of the writing process.

What can help children with handwriting difficulties?

Children need to learn to be able to write legibly in a way that is comfortable and sustainable. They need to carry out writing with increasing levels of automaticity and at a speed appropriate to the task.

Handwriting needs to be seen as supporting the writing process and where it is not automatic, vital cognitive resources which are needed for the higher level skills of composing, planning and editing, are diverted away from the content by the need to focus on the lower level of producing the written words.

If a child continues to struggle with these aspects of her handwriting to the extent that it is having an impact on her self-confidence, it may be necessary to seek referral to an occupational therapist via the child's family doctor or independently.

The following practical steps can help children who have handwriting problems in the classroom:

- Remember that left-handed writers need to have space on their left side (i.e. they should not sit with a right-handed child on their left) and should be shown how to position the paper/hold the pen to enable them to see what they are writing.

- Allow children to use different pens, lined paper, etc. as preferred.

- Provide a good role model by writing neatly yourself.

- Building in a writing practice session is one way forward (some schools do this first thing in the morning as a settling down activity): pupils copy something from the board or write over/under a given script (use a highlighter pen to write the sentence – the child can then write over it very easily). By separating the mechanical skill from the compositional skill you are taking pressure off the pupil.

- Handwriting needs to be seen as a fluent functional tool, not only for recording thoughts and feelings, but also to stimulate the generation and flow of ideas. Handwriting does need to be taught.

- For parents or teachers who are interested in learning more about handwriting, the following website has useful information: www.otility.com/articles/Pencil-Grasp-Patterns.aspx.

Tips for parents and teachers
When learning is presenting challenges, how can you help?

Much teaching in schools involves looking and listening and a child with learning differences may experience difficulties with either or both of these senses. A child's vision may be affected by difficulties with tracking, visual processing or seeing the words become fuzzy or move around. The child's hearing may be satisfactory on a hearing test, but their ability to understand, interpret and recall what is being said may be weak in a busy, noisy classroom.

Multisensory teaching uses all ways of learning – see it (visual), feel it (tactile), hear it (auditory) and move with it (kinesthetic). The following tips tap into all these ways of learning and save you from just repeating the same activity over and over. Children with learning differences need over-learning as their learning progress is rather like walking up a spiral staircase rather than straightforward steps up a ladder.

Even children with mild learning difficulties or differences will enjoy these activities!

Reading

A good indicator of whether a book is at the right level or not is if the child is unable to read five or more words on a page, it can be assumed that the book is too difficult for her. If this is a book she wants to read, don't deny her the opportunity, but read most of it for her, or see if it is available on CD from the library.

Daily reading is essential. Try shared reading where you read part and the child follows, then reads with you, then reads alone. If she gets stuck, tell her the word. Don't ask her to rely on context or pictures. You may be surprised that she can read a word on one page, and not recognize it on the next. She may be able to read 'motorway' but consistently misread 'then' or 'when'. Try to avoid showing frustration at this. The longer words are often easier for her to recall as they have concrete meaning and a stronger visual shape.

Re-reading the book helps to build familiarity and helps to reinforce understanding of the story. Reading aloud with a child helps her to understand and enjoy what she is reading and it helps develop a child's vocabulary. It also helps to read along with books on tape or CDs from the library.

Some children find that they can read a lot better when they have a tinted overlay: a plastic sheet which comes in various colours. Visual overlays can be bought quite cheaply and your child's school may be able to assess which colour is best as this differs from child to child.[3]

Spelling

Here are some tips for learning to spell in a multisensory way.

- Trace words with a pencil or pen while spelling the word out loud. Say the letter names, not their sounds and use joined writing if the child is old enough: then trace with an eraser. Get up and do five jumping jacks. Now look at the word, cover it up, write the word and check for accuracy. Give praise if right and say 'better luck next time!' if not.

---

3   An interesting website with information about this is: www.essex.ac.uk/psychology/ overlays.

- Write words down your arm as you say the letters. Try this with eyes open and eyes closed.

- While sitting on a carpet, write down each word directly onto the carpet with two fingers.

- Use magnetic letters on the refrigerator to make a word a day.

- Trace over each word at least three different times in different colour crayons so that the words look like rainbows.

- Clap your hands to each letter as you spell the words out loud.

- Type each of the words in five different fonts, colours and sizes, and display on a wall.

- Bounce a ball to each letter in the word.

- Write the words using a thick paintbrush and water on a path outside.

- Finger-paint the words.

Homework

Homework can be a frustrating and upsetting experience for children and their parents on a daily basis. Below are some tips to help make homework a more profitable experience. First of all, remember: the purpose of homework is to practise something that your child is already familiar with. If homework is too difficult, you should discuss this with the child's teacher. Don't allow your child to become frustrated because homework tasks are beyond their skills or take too long. Setting smaller amounts of work and/or allowing extra time will often help.

- Agree where and when homework gets done which is flexible enough to take into account after-school activities.

- The homework place needs to be as quiet as possible, with a cleared space for work and items required at hand, for example pens, pencils, rubber, books, etc.

- Agree the best time for your child to do her homework: she may be very tired after school as she has had to work harder because of her difficulties. She may need something to eat or drink or some free time before starting homework.

- Break homework tasks down into manageable parts. Work for short periods of time like 20 minutes, then stop for five minutes. This fools the brain into getting less tired!

- Check that your child understands what to do and read instructions to her aloud and if necessary, practise the first example or two with her.

- Help your child to come up with ideas for writing tasks and projects before she starts work. If necessary, revise vocabulary that she may need. Sometimes you may help to develop a writing plan.

- Encourage her to present work using her personal strengths — for example, she could use pictures if good at art.

- When necessary and appropriate, write for your child so that she can get her ideas on paper more accurately if this has been agreed with school.

Checking and monitoring work

- Help your child to learn editing, self-monitoring and checking skills so she can go over her own work more independently as she gets older.

- If she is slow to complete work, encourage her to use a timer and see how much work she can complete in five minutes.

- Give your child lots of praise as she completes homework tasks. Be specific about what she has done well.

Developing a child's self-esteem

When a child thinks that he is not keeping up with his peers in school, his self-confidence and feelings of self-worth can be weakened. By understanding how to support children in this respect, you can help them to cope with everyday adversities.

What is self-esteem?

Self-esteem means appreciating your own worth and importance. It means having a sense of your own value and believing in your own abilities. When children are not succeeding well in school, or feel frustrated, it is likely that their sense of self-esteem is weak or low. If they do not feel valued by their teacher, their classmates or themselves, it is easy for them to slip into a state of learned helplessness where they come to anticipate failure rather than success and lower their own expectations. There is a tendency for us all to act in ways that are consistent with what we believe about ourselves. If you don't think you can do something, you are not going to try. If you think people don't like you, you probably won't try to make them like you.

What factors influence self-esteem?

Children's self-esteem is influenced significantly by verbal and non-verbal communication with people they consider to be important such as friends, parents and teachers. Comments such as 'Good job! I like the way you helped tidy up,' only work if the person saying it has body language which supports the positive comment. Children as young as five compare themselves with others and this is related to the pride and excitement which comes from success, or the disappointment which comes with failure. Enjoyment fosters higher levels of self-esteem and motivation to be an active class participant.

People of any age with good self-esteem often:

- are 'in charge' of themselves in terms of how they feel and cope with situations

- anticipate that situations are predictable and manageable: if you coped with this test, you can cope with the next one

- perform confidently because they believe in themselves.

People of any age with poor self-esteem often:

- believe they can't change situations, it's not their fault

- think that it's about good and bad luck and because teachers or other authority figures don't like you

• don't believe that anything they do will lead to better results.

Parents and teachers can help children with low self-esteem to understand the reasons for their success or failure. Rather than let children think that their failure is a direct result of their lack of ability and that their successes are due to luck, significant adults can look to reasons for children's difficulties and provide accurate feedback about their progress. Children with low self-esteem need challenges where the difficulty increases in very small steps. This means they can begin to be more motivated through a sound understanding of the *causes* of their difficulties rather than the symptoms you can see in their work, their body language, their communication and their relationships.

Emphasize 'do's' rather than 'don'ts', setting and sticking to clear expectations and directions. When this is combined with praise which is genuine and linked to what they are doing, children will have a positive attitude towards themselves and others. Give visual as well as auditory feedback for *positive* behaviours, use lots of eye contact, say the child's name and show appreciation every time anyone does something well or worthwhile. In her book *Happy Kids, Happy You* (2009), Sue Beever has produced a toolkit of ideas to help parents speak and behave more positively with their children. It covers children's well-being and emotional health and has some useful ways to improve self-esteem. Teachers might find it useful too.

Mutual respect and other expressions self-reliance

The saying of 'please' and 'thank you' and mutual respect need to be developed so that children know they are valued. Adults need to be clear and consistent about their own values. When they feel valued, they are more able to make good decisions and to feel capable and positive about themselves, and this influences how they model behaviour to the children they interact with.

Whether a child succeeds at school is strongly linked not simply to her ability, but to her perception of her worth and whether she feels loved and nurtured. Emotional and social indicators such as feeling self-assured and interested are important, as is knowing what kind of behaviour is expected in school and social settings. A child's ability to curb the impulse to misbehave, to follow directions, and to get along with other children are all dependent on having positive feelings about herself and about the learning process.

Summary

In every classroom there are going to be children who are struggling to cope with an invisible disability. They do not achieve their potential if this barrier is not identified. This is particularly so when a child has developed strategies which mask his problems. By working very hard, he keeps his head above water, but often only a parent will recognize the stress this is causing him to experience on a daily basis. When a child's foundation for learning is shaky, its effect is felt throughout his experiences. By looking at the causes of these difficulties, rather than just the symptoms, you begin to find ways to help the child through helping him feel better about himself.

5

Vision, Visual Processing and Learning

This chapter looks at:

★ why visual problems are often not identified

★ learning difficulties associated with visual issues

★ practical strategies for helping children with visual problems

★ behavioural optometry

★ a helpful example of a vision assessment checklist

★ primitive and postural reflexes and visual problems.

Sight tests, visual processing problems and learning difficulties

Jake thinks it's normal for words to be blurry on the page. Tom has a habit of constantly blinking and needs to use his finger to keep his place when reading: his school report says he has weak concentration. Marie's teacher notices her covering her eye by leaning with her elbow on the table. Their parents say their eyes have been checked and are functioning normally.

Vision is a dynamic process that is far more complex than just being able to see clearly when looking at a stationary object, such as an eye chart. Vision involves looking at multiple stimuli that are constantly changing in time and space, and then being able to interpret the meaning and importance of those stimuli. (Kurtz 2006, p.11)

In other words, children must have both good eyesight and good visual skills to be 'fit' to learn to read and write. Many children score 20/20 eyesight on the basic eye chart, but still have poor visual skills which interfere with their ability to read, copy work and to write clearly. In fact, the quality of a child's vision and visual perception affects all aspects of their physical, intellectual, emotional and social growth.

Many children with good eyesight who have developmental delays demonstrate problems with visual perception. Children rarely realize, however, that they have a visual processing problem of this nature and their behaviours may be misinterpreted as they seem to have poor attention during reading, and may, understandably, express a dislike of reading. Parents and teachers, mistakenly believing that there is no visual problem, after a successful visit to the optician, are also likely to ignore the possibility of underlying visual causes. Adults involved with the child may therefore wrongly attribute his behaviour, learning or attitude issues to dyslexia, poor reading ability, or emotional and behavioural difficulties.

Throughout school, there are demands placed on children to become increasingly competent learners and in order to achieve this, they need to become fluent, confident readers. Reading requires, for example, the ability to learn and use knowledge of language, letter sounds, how sounds blend together and what words mean. These days most children are likely to spend much of their time watching television, playing video games, using computers (Kurtz 2006) – activities that are not very challenging in terms of making their eyes work since they do not involve shifts from looking into the distance to looking more closely, for example. Because the development of complex visual skills requires practice, the large amount of time that today's children spend on close visual work in school can result in strain to the eyes, and may contribute to delays in the development of mature visual skills (Kurtz 2006). Problems with the efficient use of vision, especially with using the two eyes together (binocular vision) to shift focus are also common in children with ADHD, dyslexia and other learning difficulties. Of course, it is possible for a child to have several challenges to their learning. They may have ADHD in addition to visual problems. Once the visual problems have been addressed, their learning differences may or may not be affected. Even when we are aware of the possibility of visual problems, these difficulties can be hard for parents and teachers to recognize for a number of reasons:

> Unfortunately...symptoms of vision difficulty can be subtle, and may fluctuate over time, so they may not be observed at the time of routine vision screenings... also, many children with vision problems fail to complain about blurred or double vision, headaches or eye-strain because they do not recognize these symptoms as problems. For many children with vision problems, this is the way their eyes have always worked so they do not realize that other children may actually see things differently. (Kurtz 2006, p.13)

Detecting problems with vision

It is important to look out for signs that a child may be struggling to see. The following section describes behaviours, symptoms, errors and difficulties that can indicate problems with vision.

Behaviours and symptoms associated with visual processing problems

- Having regular headaches.

- Complaining that their eyes hurt or text makes them dizzy.

- Sitting very close when watching the TV.

- Mannerisms such as eye poking and rubbing, squinting.

- Tilting the head or covering one eye during reading.

- Moving the head to follow a line of print, instead of moving the eyes independently of the head.

- Persistently holding books or worksheets at unusual angles such as sideways on.

- Avoidance tactics: will do anything to avoid reading.

- Difficulty concentrating during reading or other activities requiring close visual attention.

- Difficulties copying from a board.

- General difficulty with the writing process such as missing out letters from words, or words from sentences.

- Being clumsy or poorly coordinated, with poor judgement as to the distance of objects as well as difficulty throwing at a target or catching a ball.

Reading errors associated with visual problems

- Reading errors such as skipping lines, leaving out punctuation, changing the order of letters in words.

- Reads a word on one page but does not recognize it on the next.

- Inserting words or letters from the line above or below.

- Very slow reading.

- Weak understanding of what is being read: weak reading comprehension despite good vocabulary and spoken language skills.

- Difficulty more apparent when there are too many words or other images on the page.

- Difficulty in understanding the symbols used in learning other subjects involving diagrams, maps, charts or graphs.

Problems with visual tracking

Visual tracking refers to the ability to keep the eyes focused on a line in a book, and this ability is necessary for success in the classroom and in physical activities. Eye tracking skills are not fully developed until a child reaches the age of seven and children need to learn to move their eyes across a line of print and from one line to another without making mistakes. The ability to track enables a child to keep attention on the task, which is fundamentally important in terms of keeping his place in reading and being able to concentrate on the content rather than on the physical processes required to read.

Problems with fixation

Fixation is the ability to look at and focus on an object for a length of time. Fixation ability varies according to the time of day, amount of stress, and amount of time the eyes are used. At the beginning of the day, or at the beginning of reading, children may be able to focus for a while. However, as they become more tired the stress of trying to keep the eyes focused begins to affect their reading comprehension.

Problems with vision and motor development

Some children have difficulties with processing or making sense of the information that comes from their visual system. According to Cheatum and Hammond (2000) the brain does not receive the information, process it correctly or transfer it to the other sensory systems that need it for a particular action. One of the examples they give is of a child who trips every time he walks onto a mat on the floor. He appears to see the mat each time he crosses it, but for some reason the visual or proprioceptive system does not process the correct information. At a milder level, a child with visual and motor issues will be unable to hit or catch most balls, can catch a ball on the right or left side of the body, but not in the middle and is generally poorly coordinated.

What can help at home and school?

When a child has difficulties with his visual performance, it is important that the impact of this is recognized and that he is reassured that his difficulties are not related to his inborn ability or intelligence. We are using our eyes all day long and if they are not working efficiently, eye strain and frustration are to be anticipated (Kurtz 2006). Completing the checklist I include later in this chapter may help establish where the difficulties lie and this is useful information to have when seeking specialist advice from the optician or behavioural optometrist (there is more information on behavioural optometry later in the chapter too).

There are a number of practical strategies which can be put in place to make life easier for the child who has visual processing problems:

- Avoid glare on work surfaces. For example, avoid placing a computer or television screen directly in front of a window.

- Encourage children to read or do other close visual work at an eye-to-activity distance that is approximately equal to the distance between the elbow and the middle knuckles. If you lean on your elbow and bring your knuckles to your eyes, this is an easy way to judge the distance.

- Using a book rest for reading can place less stress on the eyes than reading a book that is flat on the desk because all the lines of print are at an equal distance from the eyes.

- Discourage a child from reading, watching television, or playing video games while lying sideways on the floor because this position affects the way in which the eyes work when looking at the target.

- Television should be viewed from a distance of eight to ten feet from the screen.

- If copying from the board is difficult, provide a copy of notes for the child with visual problems.

- When engaged in an extended piece of close visual work, it is advisable to take visual 'breaks' by looking up and focusing on a distant target for about ten seconds.

- Get up and move around every 15 to 20 minutes, depending on the age of the child.

(Kurtz 2006, p.76)

Another option is taking the child to see a behavioural optometrist. The following section is written by Chris Young, a behavioural optometrist based in Somerset, in the west of England. He gives his perspective on how visual difficulties may affect learning and general functioning.

Why we should be interested in behavioural optometry

CHRISTOPHER YOUNG BSC (HONS) M C OPTOM., OPTOMETRIST

Optometrists are primarily clinicians. Despite enormous strides in the understanding and knowledge of the visual system and the way it works, however, the funding and therefore the content of the basic sight test in the UK at least is the same now as it was in the late 1950s when it was first introduced.

Nevertheless, a few optometric pioneers have started to broaden the range of services they offer. For an extra fee it is now possible to receive a much more comprehensive examination, with associated advice and treatment. One of the areas these clinicians have stimulated my interest in relates to how visual problems can affect behaviour, in particular problems associated with reading.

I have lost count of how many times over the years worried parents have brought their child to me because the child appears to be experiencing problems with reading, or complains of eye rubbing, sore eyes or excessive blinking. The children generally seem unaware of a problem but why shouldn't they be, they've never known anything different?

The results of the sight test often, although not always, show the eyes to be working normally, with good distance and near vision. The eyes appear to be pointing in the same direction, work together as a pair, and the patient can struggle through the words on our near reading card. The inside of the eyes look healthy, and, in a nutshell, that's the end of the test. The advice: 'It's not the eyes, hopefully they will grow out of it' was not only disappointing for the parents but incredibly frustrating for me. The problem was present, there seemed to be a connection, but the basic sight test didn't expose the answers.

The sight test shouldn't be dismissed completely, however. With school vision screening services in this country at best patchy, then the local optometrist is the best place to start. I've had 12-year-olds come to me for their first sight test having been classified as dyslexic when all they needed was a pair of glasses and 'hey presto', problem solved. The first sight test can be performed on babies as young as three months to look for gross defects that will affect visual development, and then reviewed annually thereafter.

But for children with a problem not displaying an obvious visual defect there really was until recently nowhere else for the parents of my child patients to take them. There are now two specialist branches of optometry available to concerned parents. *Paediatric optometrists* have extended their knowledge of eye development and problems in children's eyes and use traditional examination and correction techniques, while *behavioural optometrists* take a more holistic approach and use vision therapy as well as spectacles to improve their patient's symptoms. However, this approach is controversial. In 2008 a review concluded that:

> Although there are areas where the available evidence is consistent with claims made by behavioural optometrists (most notably in relation to the treatment of convergence insufficiency, the use of yoked prisms in neurological patients, and in vision rehabilitation after brain disease/injury), a large majority of behavioural management approaches are not evidence-based, and thus cannot be advocated. (Barrett 2008)

Nevertheless, because the former discipline did not seem to offer all the answers I needed, I enrolled on a two year course on behavioural optometry run by the British Association of Behavioural Optometrists (www.babo.co.uk).

Behavioural optometry is 'a branch of optometry concerned with the diagnosis and treatment of visual problems taking into account not only the ocular history, signs and symptoms but the whole person and his or her environment' (Millodot 2000).

> It is simply a mindset, or philosophy. It encourages the observation of the behaviour of the patient. This enables the practitioner to make inferences about the patient's reaction to the test or intervention applied. These observations are made from a much more holistic perspective than the usual 'routine examination'. (Adler 2009)

After one weekend series of lectures and demonstrations I have already changed the way I examine my patients. Rather than asking if the child has a problem reading, I ask if the child enjoys reading and the response has been incredible. I either get a very positive 'yes' from the child, or an emphatic 'no'. I am now able to perform further simple tests to help evaluate whether the child's visual system would benefit from further investigation and instigate some simple therapies to start treatment, although at this point I have to start charging. (I have already performed a lot more than the basic sight test requires.)

I now realize that my knowledge of the visual system really was rudimentary, and I have barely scratched the surface of behavioural examination techniques and treatments. Reference to the BABO website will give a list of experienced practitioners dedicated to helping children and adults improve their reading, balance and spatial awareness. For some people it can be a revelation.

Visual checklists

There are many vision checklists available these days, but the problem with most of them is that it is hard to sort out whether items are checked because a child is frustrated, misbehaving, doesn't know how to read, or has other issues going on in his life. Here, an attempt has been made to narrow the questions down to those most pertinent to reading problems that are caused by vision problems and to rank each item's relative importance as well.[4]

Explanation of the checklist items

The checklist is divided into six sections, depending upon who makes the observations and when they are made.

The number at the left is intended to give you some perspective as to how important any particular observation is, with the higher numbers indicating that you should be more concerned about a vision problem.

---

4   Vision checklist and explanation of checklist items reprinted with the permission of Ian Jordan (see ontrackreading.com/the-vision-piece/vision-assessment-checklist for further explanation).

The numbers are not intended to be added up, but if your child has just a few 4s and 5s, or a lot of lower-numbered items checked, you should consider having your child examined by a developmental or behavioural optometrist.

Section 1

These observations are made by the *parent*. The first item refers to a parent having an obvious vision problem other than acuity, such as a lazy eye. However, very few parents who had a vision problem as a child actually realize that they had one.

Instead, they will remember that the early years of school were very unpleasant because they were not able to keep up with others in reading. That is why item number 2 is asked.

The third item is another way of determining whether dyslexia is running in the family.

Note: Obviously, if your child is learning to read with no problem, he is one of the lucky ones who is not being affected by a family history of dyslexia and no vision issue should be suspected unless other symptoms are noted in the last five sections of the checklist. This does *not* mean, however, that your child is not capable of passing on the genetic tendency to his or her own children.

The last two items have lower points because, by themselves, they don't necessarily indicate vision problems.

Section 2

This section covers observations made by the *child*. If your child volunteers information that he is experiencing any of these five behaviors, count yourself fortunate that he has provided you with all the information you need to justify having him evaluated by a developmental optometrist, *even if he can read as well as his peers*. These five symptoms are all strongly indicative of problems with your child's visual system, but many children won't realize they are even going on because that's the way it's always been for them. They all have 5s because they are all important on their own.

Furthermore, many children learn to read (though they might struggle at it for a bit) but still have vision problems that are blocking them from achieving their potential. If a child complains of headaches when he reads, and he has passed an eye test, it would be advisable to consider an appointment with a behavioural optometrist for further evaluation as the long term implications can affect academic success.

Section 3

In this section observations of the child are made by the parent and the behaviours tend to occur any time during the reading process, including right away when the child starts reading.

The first two sections have high numbers in front of the items because they almost always indicate vision issues. This section, assuming none of the items in the first two sections were checked, is tougher, which is why the numbers range from 1 to 5. A child who consistently covers one eye almost certainly has something going on visually and so it gets a 5. On the other hand, while a vision problem might cause a child to prefer finger tracking, a lot of younger children track print with their fingers and learn to read just fine, so it gets a 1 assigned to it.

Section 4

In this section observations of the child are made by the parent and the behaviours tend to occur after the child has been reading for at least a page or so.

These are the reading behaviours that result from an inability to sustain the effort of reading or doing other close-up work because the child's visual skills are not well developed. Here, too, the numbers reflect the importance of the behaviour being observed. The lower-numbered items might also be symptoms of other reading issues, such as having been poorly instructed and getting frustrated at not understanding how print works, for example.

These are also the behaviours that are demonstrated by a child who can often pass a standard optometric test battery easily. This is because the signs of visual discomfort don't manifest themselves right away. The child can converge his eyes on print for a time, but he can't sustain the effort. He passes your family optometrist's tests, but fails the more extensive testing done by a developmental optometrist.

Section 5

This section covers handwriting skills and should only be considered in conjunction with a child's reading problem. That is, if your child's handwriting is terrible, but he reads fine, and your family optometrist sees no problem, don't be overly concerned about items in this section. Nevertheless, children with vision issues do manifest these symptoms regularly, so this section is added for further confirmation of a vision problem.

Section 6

Frankly, this is the fall-back section. A child who has no other symptoms on this checklist, but hates to read should be seen by a developmental optometrist to rule out vision as the reason. Similarly, a very young child who just can't seem to pick up the concept of how print works, but otherwise has normal intelligence, should probably have his vision checked. The hardest referral I ever made was in just such a case. Only later did I find out that one of the parents struggled with reading in the early grades. This section is on the checklist to make sure that a vision problem is ruled out when reading problems persist and it assumes that a child has had sufficient phonics instruction as well. Children who don't understand *how* to read will manifest symptoms in this section but might not have vision problems.

If the results on the Vision Assessment Checklist suggest the existence of a vision problem, your next step should be to find the right eye-care professional to diagnose the situation.

OnTrack Reading Vision Assessment Checklist[5]

1. Parent observations (asked of parent without child present):
4 ____ Either parent had an obvious vision problem as a child
4 ____ Either parent had trouble initially learning to read in school
4 ____ Siblings of child or parents had trouble with initial reading
3 ____ Child does not read for pleasure
3 ____ Child is somewhat clumsy, bumps into things, trouble catching ball

2. Client observations (questions for client):
5 ____ Gets headaches after reading a while
5 ____ Eyes water, itch or otherwise bother when reading or soon after
5 ____ Print gets blurry
5 ____ Words sometimes double up
5 ____ Words move around on the page

3. Posture observations when reading (observed immediately):
5 ____ Occludes one eye
4 ____ Excessive head tilt, resuming after correction
3 ____ Eyes very close to page, resuming after correction
2 ____ Overall odd posture, resuming after correction
2 ____ Tracks with head movement
1 ____ Tracks with finger

4. Behavioural observations when reading (consistently observed after reading several minutes):
5 ____ Yawns, tears or cries
4 ____ Rubs eyes
4 ____ Reading pace slows noticeably over time
3 ____ Reading pace quickens after short break
2 ____ Excessive blinking
2 ____ Loses place
2 ____ Skips lines
2 ____ Skips words
2 ____ Fidgeting grows noticeably
2 ____ Avoidance tactics increase noticeably

5. Observations when writing:
3 ____ Very poor letter formation
2 ____ Words sloping away from line
1 ____ Words begun well to the right on a line

---

5   See ontrackreading.com/the-vision-piece/vision-assessment-checklist for further explanation.

6. Later behavioural observations (after five or six sessions):
5 _____ Still does not read for pleasure
4 _____ Continued failure to infer patterns in words
3 _____ Reversals of b/d persist in reading or writing

••

Why can't my child catch the ball?

The child with immature balance or retained primitive reflexes and/or visual difficulties may experience frustration in physical activities.

In order for a child to catch a ball, he needs to track it moving towards him and anticipate where to move his hands to catch it. He needs to be continually adjusting his focus, his posture and controlling the direction and speed of his movement to achieve this. For some children this can be difficult and they begin to anticipate that they will not catch the ball and give up trying.

> Remember Gemma? The little girl struggling with her reading and getting increasingly frustrated? Her grandmother heard about our work and contacted me. Gemma was assessed for neurodevelopmental delay and her scores indicated that this did not seem to be the root of her difficulties. However, it did indicate visual tracking problems and a referral to a behavioural optometrist was recommended. Although Gemma's eyesight had previously been tested by an optician, her tracking problems had not been identified. Subsequently Gemma was put on a vision therapy programme including exercises and glasses, both of which helped her reading to improve. This in turn gave her the confidence she was lacking

A child who has difficulty in kicking a ball may have immature balance and be unable to stand on one leg, whilst kicking with the other without falling over.

Children may be developmentally delayed and have a cluster of small, but detectable physical dysfunctions that are preventing them from demonstrating their intelligence in the classroom, playground and at home. In order for them to be able to function effectively, they need good posture and balance and this in turn is dependent on secure postural reflexes and the absence of primitive reflexes which can undermine their visual, vestibular and proprioceptive systems. Put simply, if the foundations of brain/body communication are not working effectively, they will disrupt the smooth functioning of higher skills, forcing the child to adopt strategies in order to learn.

As a result, these are children who may also benefit from a movement programme which targets balance and coordination. If you look back at Chapter 1, having read the checklist above, you will now be able to reflect on how a child's primitive and postural reflex profile can act to undermine their ability to perform to their potential and how it is possible to look for the causes of difficulties once the symptoms are matched more closely.

The poster below outlines how behavioural optometry may help some children.

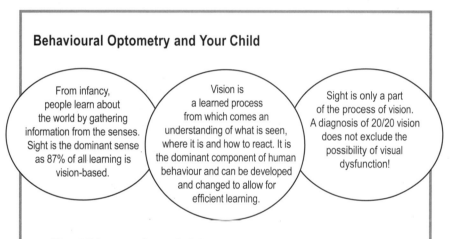

Behavioural Optometry and Your Child

From infancy, people learn about the world by gathering information from the senses. Sight is the dominant sense as 87% of all learning is vision-based.

Vision is a learned process from which comes an understanding of what is seen, where it is and how to react. It is the dominant component of human behaviour and can be developed and changed to allow for efficient learning.

Sight is only a part of the process of vision. A diagnosis of 20/20 vision does not exclude the possibility of visual dysfunction!

The children need your help!

Any student who has written language difficulties or who exhibits a significant difference in levels of ability in various subjects may be a candidate for specialized vision testing.

These factors are often most easily recognized in the classroom setting, particularly if the child is reluctant to complete close work tasks. Please be aware of symptoms of possible visual dysfunction. Identification and treatment of visual difficulty greatly increases the chances of a child's success in school. The following visual difficulties are most likely to affect learning and can be corrected with treatment options such as lenses and/or eye exercises.

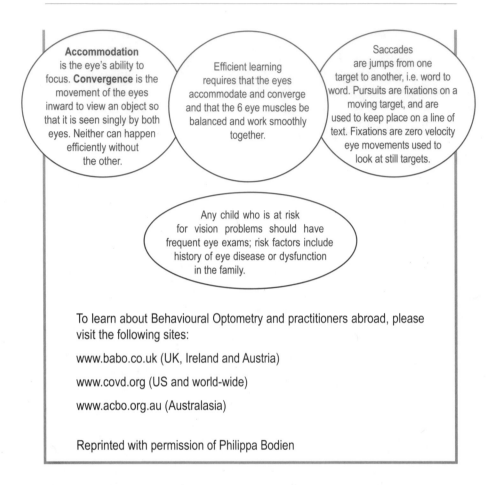

Accommodation is the eye's ability to focus. **Convergence** is the movement of the eyes inward to view an object so that it is seen singly by both eyes. Neither can happen efficiently without the other.

Efficient learning requires that the eyes accommodate and converge and that the 6 eye muscles be balanced and work smoothly together.

Saccades are jumps from one target to another, i.e. word to word. Pursuits are fixations on a moving target, and are used to keep place on a line of text. Fixations are zero velocity eye movements used to look at still targets.

Any child who is at risk for vision problems should have frequent eye exams; risk factors include history of eye disease or dysfunction in the family.

To learn about Behavioural Optometry and practitioners abroad, please visit the following sites:

www.babo.co.uk (UK, Ireland and Austria)

www.covd.org (US and world-wide)

www.acbo.org.au (Australasia)

Reprinted with permission of Philippa Bodien

Summary

Vision is more than the ability to pass a sight test. In fact, this can be misleading when it diverts attention away from the underlying visual problems and their impact on every aspect of a child's daily life. The routes for intervention and support include simple strategies which can be used in the classroom and home, as well as developmental movement programmes and referral for more extensive eye function investigations.

Hearing, Auditory Processing and Learning

This chapter looks at:

★ the importance of hearing and listening skills

★ auditory problems and receptive and expressive language development

★ causes and symptoms of hearing problems

★ symptoms of auditory processing difficulties

★ removing barriers in the classroom

★ what speech and language therapists can do

★ sound therapy and auditory stimulation programmes.

Why hearing skills are important

The ability to communicate is an essential life skill for all children – it is at the core of social interaction. Without good communication skills, children struggle to learn, to achieve in school, to make friends and to understand and communicate with the world around them. From an early age, if a child cannot clearly hear or understand instructions, she is likely to become frustrated and her behaviour may become misinterpreted as disruptive.

Children who appear to be underperforming in the classroom may be doing so for a number of reasons. In this chapter we consider how some hearing difficulties can be identified, what impact they have on learning, and how teachers and others working in schools and outside agencies can identify these auditory difficulties and make early interventions.

It is easy to underestimate how much of the information we receive about our environment comes through sound. In a busy classroom, a child has to pay attention to certain sounds while ignoring other irrelevant noises in the background. Effective listening involves more than simple 'good hearing'.

Receptive language skills developed in the pre-school phase and beyond

Receptive language – a child's *understanding* of language – develops as the child grows and is able to understand more complex communications. Receptive language is seen as the foundation for all language and communication skills and it continues to develop through the first few years at school and beyond. Receptive language (or comprehension) skills include:

- understanding words (vocabulary)

- understanding sentences and phrases

- following instructions

- understanding concepts such as colours

- understanding questions such as 'Who?'

Receptive problems can show up when a child misunderstands what is being said to her, including having difficulty following instructions or answering questions strangely. For example a child with receptive language difficulties might answer 'What did you eat for lunch today?' with 'Nowhere'. The ability to process language and to make sense of what people are saying is fundamental to our ability to understand our world and interact with it meaningfully.

It is important to remember that receptive language skills develop before expressive language skills and that many complex skills must be developed for a child to be able to express herself and understand others. Many children who have a language delay or language disorder may have a great difference between their ability to *understand language* and to *use language* socially. This can be a great source of frustration for them. Appropriate attention and listening skills need to be in place to support the development of age-appropriate receptive language skills. In building a child's language and communication skills, it needs to be remembered that many associated skills must be developed. The actual production of speech sounds must be strengthened. Listening skills of discrimination, memory and recall must be practised. Breath control and the ability to express wants, needs and experiences must be nurtured through real life experiences.

Expressive language skills

Many children who have a language delay or language disorder have a major difference in their expressive and receptive language abilities. Expressive language is generally seen as consisting of three parts:

- expressive vocabulary

- word and sentence formation

- pragmatic development: the ability to use language socially.

(Mountstephen 2010)

These three parts working together make up our ability to produce and use language. Expressive language refers to having words to describe objects, actions and feelings for example and being able to use these words in sentences and conversations, following the rules of grammar (Mountstephen 2010). Difficulties with this can show up in age-inappropriate problems with grammar, as in 'Her is mean', or vocabulary such as calling a 'giraffe' a 'horse'.

Expressive language also includes how you convey meaning to others using spoken language or non-verbal language such as gestures, facial expression, sign language and body language. A child might point or make noises instead of using words. An older child with expressive language difficulties may use single words rather than sentences. When speech and language development is delayed or disordered, it is essential to find out if the child is hearing adequately.

The role of the speech and language therapist

The role of the speech and language therapist (SLT) is to assess, advise and plan support for individuals of all ages with speech, language and communication problems so that they are able to communicate and learn to the best of their ability. Some SLTs work in schools; others are linked to specialist facilities. They may work directly with individuals and groups or they may advise others about appropriate programmes of support and methods of practice. There is often a waiting list for speech and language therapy appointments; this may be due to a large number of children being referred or there may be a shortage of therapists in a particular area or field of work.

If your child has seen a speech and language therapist in school it is always beneficial to arrange a meeting with them. They will find it helpful to learn the information you can give about early development, your child's listening, speech and language at home, their interests and abilities and your main concerns. Do let the school know when you are able to attend a meeting with the therapist and teachers to discuss any planned support, and discuss how this can be followed up at home. Be sure to arrange a review meeting before you leave.

The difference between listening and hearing

One reason a child may *appear* to have learning difficulties is that she cannot understand fully what the teacher is saying to her and then act quickly to correctly interpret the meaning of what has been said. Socially she may withdraw as she struggles to follow interactions with other children. To become a good listener, we need to be able to 'zoom in' on information, but also to 'zoom out', or filter out irrelevant background information.

Good listeners hear all sounds clearly and can focus and concentrate. They are not distracted by other sensory information. Poor listeners, on the other hand, do not have these abilities and so often their only strategy is to tune out. Behavioural problems are often the result of misunderstandings as a child with auditory problems has to work harder to understand what is being said. It is like learning a foreign language for us.

Hearing is a passive process and listening is an active process. However, good hearing is the foundation of good listening. We can have excellent hearing, but be poor listeners. Poor listeners have poor development of understanding, don't follow instructions and may have poor friendship skills. They can get labelled as naughty and have problems listening to group or class instructions. In their book, *Learning to Listen to Learn* (2005), White and Evans stress the importance of attention and listening. They provide a specific programme on how to listen which helps teachers to become more aware of the listening process and how to adapt their teaching to the needs of individual pupils. According to them their programme has been used successfully in a number of secondary and primary schools with 100 per cent positive feedback from the teachers involved (White and Evans 2005, p.8).

When hearing is a problem

There are a number of possible social, environmental and biological or medical reasons why a child's communication seems to be delayed or there are difficulties. Some children with hearing loss may be wrongly thought to have an attention disorder or learning problem, or to be a poor student with behavioural issues because their auditory problems have not been recognized. Possible causes of hearing problems are:

- *Repeated ear infections*, which can have a long-term impact and implications beyond the period of the infection. One reason for conductive hearing loss is Otitis Media, commonly known as 'glue ear'. It is very common in young children and is the most common cause of poor hearing in children. It can be difficult to spot because there may not be any obvious symptoms although it often follows an ear infection or a cold. Many children with glue ear get better on their own, usually within a few months. However, some children get glue ear for long periods and their hearing is affected for substantial periods of time, even when there are no apparent symptoms. Fluid can remain in the ear for up to several months following an infection, causing difficulties in discriminating sound.

- *Problems with pregnancy and/or birth,* which can cause developmental delay including to the auditory system.

- A *specific medical syndrome* or disorder.

- A *family-related condition.*

- A *lack of early stimulation* and good quality interaction.

The symptoms of hearing loss may include:

- being inattentive

- talking too loudly and listening to the TV at a high volume

- mispronouncing words

- being unsettled at school

- 'tuning out' due to repeated experiences of changes in the intensity of auditory signals

- problems working independently due to missed or mis-heard spoken instructions

- delayed reactions to sounds or instructions

- over-sensitivity to loud or sudden noises

- poor speech and language ability

- poor balance.

As a result of hearing problems children are likely to develop language skills more slowly than their peers. In the long term, children with hearing problems will experience difficulties at home and school. These include:

- frustration, peer rejection and lack of confidence in communicating

- being less likely to initiate conversation

- playing alone

- being less liked by others in the class

- shyness in younger children

- low self-esteem in older children.

A child with hearing loss will experience these difficulties more as time progresses. It is therefore important that steps are taken as early as possible to address the child's problems.

Practical strategies for parents and schools

There is an intricate relationship between hearing and listening and it is always essential, as previously stated, to check that the child is hearing adequately as the first step in any assessment process. Due to this complex interlinking of hearing and listening, a child may pass a functional hearing test, but still not have good listening skills. A child needs to be given the time she needs to express what she wants to say without adults necessarily finishing her sentences for her. Children need to be confident that adults are interested in them and want to listen to them. By becoming comfortable with a listening approach, you give the child the message that what she wants to say is valued. Children also need to be aware of why they are listening. They need to be made aware of what to focus on, what is relevant and what can be ignored.

Communication relies upon skills such as taking turns, listening and retaining information and monitoring one's own understanding. If a child has even quite mild learning difficulties, listening with good concentration and responding appropriately can lead to a sense of anxiety which in turn contributes to more anxiety – followed by a tendency to switch off or to engage in distractible behaviour which then brings her to the attention of the teacher for the wrong reasons.

Tips for classroom organization

- Taking into account critical factors such as the acoustics of the room in terms of noise level and reverberation can be helpful as a first step. In general, a self-contained and structured environment is more effective for children with auditory difficulties than large, open plan areas.

- When thinking about the best place for children with auditory problems to sit, consider the ease with which they can see you as well as hear you as they may be using lip-reading and 'reading' your body language.

- A child with hearing or listening problems should sit away from areas of environmental noise such as doorways and hallways as she is less able to ignore peripheral noise than other children. By providing a quiet study area which has a low level of auditory and visual instructions, an older child can work without distraction and where barriers to concentration are minimized.

Practical strategies for teaching children with listening and hearing difficulties

- Provide a visual back-up such as a prompt sheet or visual prompts on the board. All children benefit from a multisensory approach to learning as this allows them to obtain input through more of their senses and this supports weak auditory abilities.

- Pre-teach specific vocabulary.

- Gain the child's attention directly before giving instructions to the class or group, facing them.

- Check that she has understood, or rephrase the instruction if necessary. It is easy for teachers to be misled into thinking a child has understood if she nods in response to a question about whether she knows what to do. Sometimes children stop asking for help as they have been made aware that teachers are frustrated by their 'constant' asking for instructions to be repeated. They are trying to listen, but are failing to take in the information effectively. This can quickly lead to frustration for the child, teacher and family. Repeat the instructions rather than rephrasing them. The child will be able to fill in the portions of the message that were missed first time. If information is rephrased, however, the child now has an entirely new message to decode, with new missing pieces to figure out. If this does not seem to be working, think about whether it is possible to break the information down into smaller chunks.

- Keep instructions simple and concise, delivered at a measured (i.e. not fast) rate. Speak clearly.

- Use a 'buddy system' by negotiating with a classmate to assist in supporting the child's focus.

- Avoid standing in front of windows where your face will go into shadow and make it difficult for children to pick up facial clues.

- Repeat what a child has said – a child with 'glue ear' will not hear what other children say in group work and a good strategy involves repeating these comments back to the class as a whole.

- A useful guide to support parents and teachers can be found in Appendix III.

The following case study is included to illustrate how complex it can be for a child's needs to be successfully identified and effectively managed. It was written by Toby's mother and conveys her perception of her son's experiences and the family's attempts to help him succeed. The main point is that there is no one clear reason or diagnosis to explain why a child is struggling, and children with one difficulty will often have others.

TOBY AND HIS FAMILY'S EXPERIENCE OF HEARING PROBLEMS

Toby's parents first spotted that he had hearing problems at six months and the midwife spent a little time with him and advised them to contact the doctor immediately. At nine months he was referred for a hearing test, which he failed. Over the next couple of years, Toby had many hearing tests, all of which he failed.

When he started speaking, Toby's parents noticed that although he had an excellent understanding and well-developed vocabulary for his age, he was having problems forming his words, he didn't seem able to pronounce basic sounds, so he was referred to a speech therapist by the time he was three. She gave Toby some exercises which helped a little, but his parents did not see as much progress as they had been led to expect. When he was four and due to start school, still with significant difficulties, they went back to the family doctor again and this time they were told that Toby would need grommets, but the waiting list to see the consultant was very long.

Deciding that this was too long to wait, they tightened their belts, forfeited any luxuries and went private. They saw the consultant the next week, who was able, because of a cancellation, to get him into the children's hospital within the month. The next few months saw Toby becoming aware, for the first time, of sounds such as a bird tweeting, traffic in the distance: the list was endless.

Over the following years, Toby made good progress with few absences from school due to ear infections. As he passed up the school, however, it seemed increasingly apparent to his parents that his school had problems distinguishing between bouts of poor hearing and what they perceived as poor concentration and off-task behaviour.

Naughty or misunderstood

Toby's parents continue to feel that Toby's teachers, SENCO and Head do not take his disability seriously enough and have considered taking him out of the last two terms at his primary school. An educational psychology assessment which they paid to have carried out confirmed that Toby is a bright boy who is under-achieving. The school's perception is that he is not concentrating, easily distracted and does not need extra support as he does not meet their criteria for support. In other words, he is doing 'well enough'. The parents thus continue with what they see as a battle against the school.

The educational psychologist had recommended that I assess Toby to see whether he would benefit from a neurodevelopmental delay programme. A detailed assessment confirmed that Toby did have both retained primitive reflexes and under-developed postural reflexes. Toby followed the INPP programme for a year and he was reassessed at regular intervals. Whereas his hearing difficulties have persisted, his reflex profile has improved significantly and this has led to improvements in his posture, balance and his emotional stability.

Toby is now looking forward to starting his new school in September, where he has already been asked to join a gifted and talented sports programme and where the learning support unit have already met with him and with his parents to plan for his learning needs.

Auditory processing problems

Auditory processing disorder (APD) results from impaired neural function and is characterized by poor recognition, discrimination, separation, grouping, localization or ordering of non-speech sounds. It does not solely result from a deficit in general attention, language or other cognitive processes (BSA 2007).

> Most of us hear well and don't give much thought to how we hear. Hearing starts with a very complex set of actions within the outer, middle and inner ear. These actions send the sounds to our brain, and our brain interprets them so we can understand. For example, it tells us the whistling we hear is a bird singing. This is what we call LISTENING. The medical term for it is AUDITORY PROCESSING. When a child's ears are working well, but the child cannot understand the sounds they hear, the child may have an 'auditory processing disorder'. (MRC Institute of Hearing Research 2004)

While some children may only need support at a fairly general level in order to move forward, others may need more specific input at an individual level.

Symptoms and signs of auditory processing disorder

A child with APD is easily distracted by noises which other children can ignore such as a dog barking, a clock ticking or people walking past. Distractibility is often said to be a hallmark of APD, but it is also a hallmark of many other disorders such as ADHD. A child with ADHD may be distracted because her mind wanders elsewhere or because a new thought or event has occurred which has distracted her away from the task at hand. However, for the child with APD, the distractibility arises from the way in which noise or competing speech interferes with the ability to understand what is being said (Bellis 2002). She is unable to listen to one speaker (the teacher) when others are talking at the same time, even though she is concentrating fully. Bellis also states that it is difficult to tease out what is causing the distractibility as the two disorders frequently co-occur.

Many of the symptoms of APD are similar to those of other disorders such as dyslexia, ADHD and language impairment. Difficulties hearing speech against background noise, following instructions presented verbally, language difficulties, erratic attention and academic concerns can be observed in many children, which is why a thorough, multi-disciplinary investigation is needed to determine the cause of the presenting problems.

Many children will have difficulty paying adequate attention to what they hear and may have delayed listening skills. The British Society of Audiology recommends that a diagnosis of APD (or atypical development) should only be made by a specialist multi-disciplinary team including an audiologist, psychologist, specialist teacher and speech and language therapist.

A range of professionals have developed an interest in and understanding of auditory processing. In many areas the first referral will be to an SLT. There may also be a specialist language teacher or a teacher of the hearing impaired who has an interest in classroom acoustics, assessment of auditory processing and planning support.

When to seek support

Your child's family doctor will be able to refer him to an SLT, and in the UK parents or carers have the right to contact speech and language therapy services directly through the NHS Trust. There is no lower age limit for referring children for speech and language therapy assessment and some children with complex needs will have been receiving support since shortly after birth. Services will vary though in the age at which they will accept referrals.

What can help at school

Minor improvements can usually be made in most classroom situations which can make a big difference to the acoustic quality of the classroom. This can increase the learning capacity of the child with APD and greatly improve her sense of well-being.

At a classroom level

- Minimize general classroom noise levels so that there is less distraction. Background music will tend to distract the child from focusing on the teaching or learning activity.

- Help the child to develop strategies to listen and remember instructions and information.

- Keep the child away from traffic areas in the classroom and open doors.

- The Auditory Integration Institute has a lot of useful information for teachers and parents.

- Consider the possibility of a seat or desk location in which the child can both hear and see the teacher and the board easily and which is where they do as much of their work as possible. Proximity to the teacher also allows the teacher to monitor the child's auditory processing and general behaviour more closely and to better establish a personal and supportive relationship.

Children often feel they are stupid or there is something very wrong with them if they are unable to listen when others can, or don't understand or forget instructions. An explanation about their difficulties often comes as a huge relief, and once people understand that it is not just a case of listening more carefully, or trying harder, everyone can contribute to making the child's life easier.

In group or individual sessions

- Consider how individual or small group teaching or therapy could be improved or tweaked to better suit a child's specific difficulties. Understanding the nature of a child's profile of strengths and difficulties is important in order to guide intervention at this level.

What to do if existing strategies aren't working

When classroom accommodations and strategies at home and school are not sufficient, further advice should be sought. In the next section, Camilla Leslie and Diana Crewdson, both experienced speech and language therapists, provide information about further options for intervention.

Sound therapy and auditory stimulation programmes

CAMILLA LESLIE, SPECIALIST SPEECH AND LANGUAGE THERAPIST, NATIONAL DIRECTOR OF JOHANSEN INDIVIDUALISED AUDITORY STIMULATION, UK AND DIANA CREWDSON, SPECIALIST SPEECH AND LANGUAGE THERAPIST

While sound therapy is a generic term for the use of sound to improve health and well-being, some sound therapies have been specifically developed as a tool to stimulate auditory attention and efficient listening skills. These are now referred to as auditory stimulation programmes and are used by a range of health and education professionals, including doctors, psychologists, occupational, speech and developmental therapists and teachers.

Six main auditory stimulation programmes are used in Britain. They have been developed in Europe and the US and are used in many parts of the world. Two are mainly centre based (The Tomatis Method and Auditory Integration Training) and four are mainly home based (Johansen Individualised Auditory Stimulation, Samonas Auditory Stimulation, The Listening Programme and Therapeutic Listening). All involve listening to music-based stimulation through good quality headphones.

The rationale for these programmes is based on our understanding of neural plasticity; this describes the way pathways in the central nervous system develop in speed and efficiency as a result of consistent stimulation, so that we can process information or react with ease and fluency (Phillips 2001). It also draws on the body of research which describes the effect of different elements of music on attention, discrimination and mood (Leeds 2001) and the links between the processing of music and language (Gilmor 1999; Miranda and Ullman 2007).

The centre-based programmes have been in use since the mid-twentieth century. Home-based programmes have developed as a result of high quality personal listening equipment being readily available. They bypass the cost and inconvenience of travelling to specialist centres, and enable listening in a relaxed and familiar environment at home or school. They provide the same overall amount of stimulation spread over a longer period. Follow-up studies (in publication) suggest that gradual stimulation produces changes to listening behaviour that are stable over time.

Johansen Indivualised Auditory Stimulation has many features in common with other programmes and is also the only form of home- or school-based stimulation where the music can be individualized for each client. We will focus on this programme, which was developed in Denmark and is now used in over twenty countries worldwide.

Clients listen for ten minutes daily over eight to twelve months. The programme sits well alongside everyday learning and other interventions such as therapy or specialist teaching. The programme is flexible, some children listen independently at home, others listen alongside an adult, some young children with immature listening skills listen to the simplest music in groups in school to support their development in the infant classes.

The Johansen IAS music has been specially designed to gently change and organize how a person listens. It helps the noticing, discrimination and organization of incoming sound, particularly speech. Listening becomes easier because less effort is required to process incoming speech which supports attention, particularly in background noise such as class group work, stamina for increased comprehension and motivation. Parents and teachers also report changes in confidence and self-esteem when children follow the programme.

A Johansen IAS programme is planned and monitored by a trained provider who will have an appropriate professional background. They will select assessments according to the client's age and ability, using checklists, observation, auditory processing measures and listening audiometry. This enables them to select the music used by each client and decide how it may be customized according to their pattern of laterality and response to different sound frequencies.

There is, as with most interventions, variation in how children respond, but very few fail to enjoy their programme and a majority demonstrate benefits that transfer to function at home and school. Feedback from parents, teachers and children includes:

> 'H's (autistic spectrum) communication has changed since he started the programme, he is now able to talk about the same thing for several exchanges and we can really chat together.'

> 'M (post trauma language difficulties) is so much calmer, he doesn't need to get into our bed every night any more.'

> 'D (dyslexic) can listen while doing something now. We really notice this when fishing together, he doesn't have to stop and turn round every time I speak to him.'

> 'I am convinced that the Johansen IAS programme has made a significant contribution to our improved foundation stage results and the ease with which pupils handle early sound work in literacy (teacher)'

> 'J (language difficulties) gets out his Johansen IAS music, listens and marks his checklist all by himself. It is the first thing he has done so independently in school.'

> 'Now I can hear when Mummy calls anywhere in the house!'

> 'I like it, it makes me feel calm so I don't worry.'

Further information on auditory stimulation programmes, including providers and provider training can be found on the websites listed in the 'Useful Resources' section, Appendix IV.

Summary

It is always vitally important to check that a child who is having problems in school or in the wider world is not experiencing undetected hearing difficulties. These can be relatively mild or intermittent and therefore often go undetected on hearing tests. When this is the case, it is advisable as a parent or teacher in frequent contact with the child to use the information in this chapter to make some judgements about whether there is a case for further investigations of auditory difficulties. There are a number of ways in which classrooms and teaching strategies can be adapted and further steps which can be taken to help. Multi-sensory learning has long been established as the best way to reach all learners more effectively.

7

How a Psychologist Can Help

Elvie Brown, Educational Psychologist

Introduction to the educational psychologist's role

Life can soon become difficult and complicated for a child if he doesn't keep pace with his peers in any aspect of his development. Whatever the reason for this, the impact can be significant for the child and have far-reaching consequences in terms of his education and emotional well-being. Something which may begin as a small delay or difficulty in learning, socializing or physical ability can rapidly be compounded by the child's response to this difficulty. There are issues around how the child copes with frustration, disappointment or disapproval. Then there is the added complication of parental and teachers' responses. These factors all serve to impinge on the child's ability to cope and to overcome his difficulties. Factors such as his emotional resilience and his self-esteem also play a part in the impact of all these compound difficulties. Each child is inherently different and consequently his response to his difficulty varies.

Understanding a child as part of a complex social system, disentangling issues around learning, emotions and behaviour is a challenge. Simple quick-fix solutions rarely exist. The first step towards change and resolution is always knowledge and understanding. The educational psychologist is in a unique position to shed light on a number of these factors and to prescribe a course of action for the child. The intervention from an educational psychologist frequently gives insight into the nature of the child's difficulties that will facilitate a change and lead to improvements in the child's learning and consequent performance.

An educational psychologist has training in teaching, education, child psychology, child development, emotion and behaviour. The educational psychologist can analyse the nature and extent of the student's difficulty and examine in depth the impact of the student's learning experiences in relation to his current difficulties and tease out where remediation should be directed and what form that help might take. An educational psychologist can also act as a consultant to schools, providing an opportunity to advise on students' difficulties, remedial and therapeutic techniques.

Why see an educational psychologist?

A referral to an educational psychologist is rarely the first step when concerns are raised about a child's performance. It is usual for the student's teachers to implement a remedial programme initially and to monitor progress closely. This work is often noted by the school and should be thoroughly discussed with the student's parents. Parents should also check out any medical issues and hearing and eyesight should always be checked as described in the earlier chapters of this book. After a suitable period of time has lapsed the student's progress should be assessed. If this intervention has failed to effectively remediate learning, behavioural or emotional issues or if the student's profile remains confusing in some manner then an educational psychologist can be called in to address the issues to hand, provide a thorough analysis and prescribe further appropriate remedial action.

The educational psychologist will explore a range of factors. He or she will take a developmental history and check on early experiences of schooling. She will also explore the student's important relationships, later school experience and teachers' inputs. She will assess the child utilizing a number of recourses aimed to provide a comprehensive overview of a child's cognitive profile, current attainments, behaviour and emotional factors where necessary. She will spend time learning about the child from the teacher's perspective and from the parents' perspective. She will empathize with the child and try to gain insight into his view of the world, how he sees himself as a learner, as a member of his class, school and family.

The educational psychologist is in a unique position to examine all the possible reasons for a student's failure to thrive at school. As an independent professional she addresses the situation with fresh eyes and without prejudice. She will take on board the views of parents and teachers, but the child is the main focus. The psychologist is not only looking to evaluate the child's difficulties but is also looking for a way in to create the momentum for change in the child's learning or behaviour.

Types of concerns

It is usual for a child to be referred to an educational psychologist following parental or school concerns about a child's progress at school. These concerns can be multifaceted. Most commonly the student is experiencing difficulties with learning, emotional problems or behavioural issues. Children can also be referred to an educational psychologist at a pre-school level. At this stage referrals can be from health professionals such as paediatricians or speech therapists. The main focus for most educational psychologists is with children of school age. Parents can refer a child directly to an educational psychologist without going through alternative professionals. This is more common when the parent is opting to use a private educational psychologist rather than one employed by the local authority.

The following lists are of the most common types of concerns expressed by teachers and parents and are the most likely reasons for referrals to an educational psychologist. This is by no means a comprehensive list but hopefully provides an insight into the kinds of difficulties students present with at the point of assessment.

Learning difficulties

- Reading/writing/spelling difficulties; dyslexia.
- Coordination/organization/perception problems; dyspraxia.
- Maths difficulties.

- Concentration and attention issues, visual or verbal.
- Communication difficulties.
- Speech and language issues.
- Hearing and auditory attention difficulties.
- Autistic spectrum difficulties.

Behavioural difficulties

- Disruptive behaviour in the classroom, at home or in school in general.
- Anger and aggressive behaviour issues.
- Social skills difficulties/autistic spectrum difficulties.
- ADHD/ADD.
- Withdrawal or communication issues.
- Difficulties with relationships – either peer relationships, family relationships or teacher/pupil relationships.

Emotional issues

- Difficulties with stress and stress management.
- Depression.
- Control issues.
- Anxiety disorders.
- Self-esteem issues.

How an educational psychologist's assessment works

The stages of the educational psychologist's assessment process are outlined below.

Reason for referral

The first step is always to look for the presenting issues, to acknowledge the concerns of the parents, student and the teachers involved.

Gathering background information

Background information is gathered about the student from all parties concerned. This includes a developmental history, medical history, social and family factors and information from and about school. It is always useful to have information from the child's teachers and recent school reports. It is important to have details of any remedial intervention which has already been implemented with the student.

Undertaking individual assessment

An educational psychologist is likely to spend time with the student concerned on an individual basis. Work carried out at this stage can vary according to the nature of the presenting issue, the amount of time available to the educational psychologist and the way in which an educational psychologist has arranged to work with a school. Local authority and private educational psychologists can vary in their practice at this stage. A full assessment might include any combination of the following:

- observation of the student in class
- structured interview with the student, which might include any combination of the following:
    - cognitive testing
    - literacy testing
    - maths testing

- ◦ emotional profiling

- ◦ personality profiling

- ◦ behavioural profiling

- ◦ learning styles profiling.

The student is closely observed throughout the assessment, and through interaction and appropriate feedback the process allows a great deal of insight into the student's learning style and personality factors that might influence his response to difficulties in the classroom. The process should be cathartic for the student, providing an opportunity for him to express his own thoughts and feelings about himself, to appreciate his strengths and weaknesses and to gain insight into his own learning styles. Through this it is hoped that students will become ready and able to adapt to altered expectations and begin to facilitate their own self-improvement.

Tests an educational psychologist may use to aid the assessment process

The educational psychologist has a variety of testing methods that she or he can use during her or his work with the child.

Cognitive testing

Psychologists can use a range of tests to explore a student's *intellectual potential* and *cognitive* make up. These include verbal reasoning tests, memory tests, perceptual reasoning tests, spatial and processing tests. The most commonly used test is the WISC-IV (Wechsler Intelligence Scale for Children, Fourth Edition). Parents will often receive reports with test scores and an interpretation. Psychologists look for a number of factors when using these tests particularly the overall ability range, and variations between the subtests. These features are usually explained in depth on the reports. Suffice to say that where the discrepancies between the various clusters of scores are found, if significant these can be helpful in understanding the nature of a student's difficulty. For example:

1. If there is a significant difference between verbal and non-verbal ability this can suggest:

    (a) a language issue, if verbal functioning is low, or

    (b) an executive functioning difficulty or dyspraxia if non-verbal functioning is low.

2. If tests measuring memory skills are comparatively low this can be linked to auditory processing issues and dyslexia.

3. If tests measuring processing skills are low this can be linked to writing and spelling issues or specific visual problems.

There are many clusters of results that are associated with various educational and behavioural issues. A psychologist is required to interpret the results.

Schools often undertake cognitive testing which they administer. The main difference between these tests is that the school tests are either paper and pencil tests or completed on the computer. Many students with learning difficulties find these testing situations similar to school-based tests and therefore the difficulties they encounter with school exams emerge when completing these tests. The psychologists' tests are individually administered meaning that each test is fully explained to the student and points can be clarified where necessary. Also, the psychologist is able to gain considerable insight into the student's learning style from the way in which he tackles the various subtests.

Literacy tests

Literacy tests are likely to be very similar to the tests carried out by teachers, particularly where the school has a strong learning support department. The educational psychologist usually likes to do these kinds of tests to examine the way in which the student operates when reading and writing. She can elicit a great deal of diagnostic information from which she can work out the most appropriate form of remedial intervention required for the student.

There are many different types of literacy tests and each one provides a unique insight into the student's difficulties. The following areas are usually covered:

- word reading

- comprehension

- speed of reading

- spelling

- handwriting

- phonological awareness.

Maths tests

Typically maths testing revolves around looking at numeracy skills. Mental maths is usually tested but this can form part of the cognitive tests as it often reflects a student's level of working memory skill. Mathematical reasoning is also tested. Most tests evaluate basic maths skills rather than higher level maths.

Profiling

Profiling tests look at emotional and behavioural factors and learning styles in more depth. They include self-reporting from the students and insights from teachers and parents. They have simple statements that the individual has to judge himself against usually by ticking an appropriate box or by giving a number value to stress how true a specific statement is to him. The results provide a picture of how students perceive themselves and how others view them. They give some measure of the seriousness of specific emotional and behavioural issues or reflect on personality or learning styles.

These profiles are usually easy to complete and students can prefer them to responding to a battery of questions. They provide a useful point for discussion and the accuracy of these personal assessments can be checked by clarifying with the students their intended meanings when compiling their responses.

Considering school-based factors

An analysis of school-based factors is usually incorporated as part of the assessment. It is always useful to consider the student as part of a school system. The insights from teachers and even school reports can reveal a story of how the child is perceived within the context of his learning environment. Schools and teachers can vary enormously as to how well they deal with students who present with learning or behaviour difficulties. A student who might be regarded as a serious problem in one educational environment may not be so regarded in another school. This kind of variation can affect the child's self-esteem and self-image. It can also influence how the teachers respond to the difficulty. For example, a student with, say, mild dyslexia may be in a school where there are a high proportion of students with severe and complex learning and behaviour issues and a mild presentation of difficulty within that environment may not be considered a priority. Within another school system the child with this kind of profile might be given individual support by specialist teachers and all the staff may be sympathetic to his situation and modify their teaching accordingly. The educational psychologist will take these factors into account when advising both a school and parents on how best to proceed with an individual student. The school's attitude and ethos towards students who have learning issues has a significant bearing on the success of any remedial interventions. The educational psychologist is in a position to influence the teaching staff and provide support and advice to them in a way that will benefit the child concerned.

Feedback and reports

Feedback is best delivered face-to-face with parents and teachers. It is usually given immediately following the student assessment. It often comprises a summary of the test findings and the general conclusions of the assessment. The educational psychologist should then go on to make suggestions and recommendations as to how best to proceed given the student's school and home circumstances.

The educational psychologist usually provides a report of the assessment. This gives details of all the factors that emerge through the process of the assessment and should summarize the key recommendations.

Likely outcomes

It has already been highlighted that a student can present with a variety of different issues at the outset of an assessment. It is, however, usual that one particular factor dominates at the point of referral. The assessment should explore a range of factors. For example many students who are referred because of behavioural issues often emerge with a significant learning difficulty. Emotional factors can also be the result of learning issues and vice-versa. The educational psychologist is the one professional who should explore and acknowledge the interplay between emotions, behaviour and learning. The child is viewed as part of school system and a family, his presenting difficulty and the likely outcome can depend upon the flexibility and resourcefulness within those systems.

Following this comprehensive evaluation of the student the educational psychologist should be able to give direct feedback to all concerned and map out a way to manage the difficulty with recommendations for teaching interventions, therapeutic programmes or behaviour management programmes.

The assessment serves to pull together all the relevant factors concerning a child and map out a route for change. The educational psychologist acts as a catalyst for change. The length of involvement of the educational psychologist with a child and family varies according to the type and severity of the difficulties encountered. An individual assessment can range from a brief encounter to a few hours. An ongoing involvement is more common with behavioural or emotional issues; here the educational psychologist can provide a number of further sessions where the focus moves from assessment to intervention.

With learning issues the educational psychologist is likely to suggest the type of remedial intervention required and to recommend a suitable course of action. The outcomes for intervention are most successful when the educational psychologist has a close relationship with the specialist teacher within the school and has an opportunity to speak directly to the teachers concerned. If this kind of feedback can be given directly after the assessment then all parties involved receive a full and comprehensive appraisal of the child's issues and the best way to help the student move forward. A feedback session at the end of the assessment with parents and teachers allows for points of clarification and discussion. A report summarizing the assessment then follows at a later date and provides a formal record of the assessment.

SARAH (AGED 7)

REASON FOR REFERRAL

Sarah was referred following school and parental concern about her reading development.

DEVELOPMENTAL HISTORY

At the point of assessment a developmental history was taken. There were no significant issues in Sarah's early years but she was presenting some early problems with articulation and she did not receive any speech therapy at the time. In all other aspects her development had been perfectly within the average range and had met expectations. Sarah was a well coordinated student during her early years having no presenting issues with gross or fine motor control. Her play skills developed normally and she was socially adaptive.

SCHOOL FACTORS

Sarah presented as a verbally engaging student, but rather restless. She is regarded as a very sociable, helpful student within the classroom, being very responsive and engaging. Having said that, she can be inclined to daydream, particularly when working independently or when listening to instructions.

In reception class at school (aged 4½) Sarah was articulate and adaptive to teachers' expectations. The impression of Sarah from her teachers at that time was that she was an able student who was unlikely to have any presenting difficulties with her learning.

In Year 1 (aged 5½) Sarah had mastered some basic skills reasonably well, particularly in maths. She had a few sight words and could read basic script. Her maths was developing very well. However, her teachers began to note that she was struggling to retain instructions. She also kept reversing letters and numbers. Moreover, Sarah could become quite fidgety and easily distracted when asked to engage in written work tasks. She was struggling with letter formation and with her general writing skills.

By Year 2 Sarah's parents were beginning to show some concerns. Sarah (now 6½ years old) was not really retaining sight words and her word attack skills were lower than one might expect given the perception of Sarah's ability, and she was also struggling to master spelling skills. She could often learn spellings for a test but would be unable to remember them when required to do so at a later date.

Sarah's school teacher at the time thought that she was rather immature in her general presentation and tended to be overly social rather than applying herself to tasks at hand. She was easily distracted within the classroom. The general feeling expressed by teachers was that although she had some mild difficulties, she needed time to develop further.

FAMILY FACTORS

Her parents were not sure about the teachers' appraisal of Sarah. At home she was beginning to resist school-based tasks, particularly literacy activities, but would engage in all other types of activities without any difficulty. Her problems with getting down to reading and writing tasks were beginning to cause some friction between Sarah and her mother. Also, Sarah's younger sister Amy who was in reception class was already beginning to make better progress with reading and this was causing some further difficulties in the family. The school agreed to give Sarah a boost to her reading skills and work on a basic phonic-based programme. After three months of this initiative little progress had been made with Sarah.

THE ASSESSMENT

A formal assessment was conducted with Sarah. Sarah impressed as a student who was reasonably articulate and could speak openly about her school experiences. She was aware that she was struggling with aspects of the curriculum. Although Sarah is only 7 years old she was already conscious of learning issues, particularly with literacy, and showed some misgivings about her place within the class. She was similarly aware that she has strengths and had capitalized upon these.

Sarah readily engaged in all the tasks required of her through the assessment. It was very interesting to observe Sarah through the process of the assessment. First, she responded quickly and easily to all verbal items. She concentrated very well through all the cognitive activities and had no difficulties with learning new things. However, when we began to work on the literacy-based issues her demeanour changed. She became quite restless, fidgety and kept trying to engage in general conversation. She displayed a significant repertoire of work avoidance strategies at this point. She was not inappropriate in her actions but it was evident that she was struggling with the task in hand.

The assessment explored many complex facets with Sarah but in essence revealed the following:

Cognitive factors

Sarah's overall ability presented within the top 10 per cent.

Verbal reasoning	Above average
Perceptual reasoning	Above average
Working memory	Below average
Speed of processing	Low average

Her weaknesses were in the following areas:

- Short-term memory
- Sequencing
- Speed of processing

Basic skills

Word reading	Standard score 85
Reading comprehension	Standard score 96
Speed of reading	Standard score 90
Non word reading	Standard score 82
Spelling	Standard score 86
Handwriting	6 wpm
Mathematical reasoning	Standard score 110

Word reading

Sarah was showing marked difficulties with her word reading facility. She struggled to decode complex polysyllabic words. She had a bank of sight words she could read accurately but was rather slow as she approached complex polysyllabic words. She often read a word on the basis of the overall visual presentation rather than decoding sub-components, thus she was frequently substituting a whole word with an alternative word that had a very similar visual presentation.

Reading comprehension

Sarah was struggling to read and process information simultaneously. She read rather slowly and when she finished a passage she had to re-read in order to be able to answer questions accurately. Sarah's knowledge of phonic-based strategies was poor for her age. She has acquired the ability to identify c-v-c words and initial and final consonant blends. She was however struggling to decode medial components of a word. Beyond this level her phonological awareness was limited.

Spelling

Sarah had acquired a number of sight words that she could spell accurately. She was fluent with these words and would use them on a regular basis in her structured pieces of writing at school. However, when she moved out of her comfort zone she often produced irregular letter combinations or bizarre spellings. Her work was not always phonetically regular.

Handwriting

With handwriting Sarah was very slow to produce written work. She can formulate her letters correctly and could produce a neat rounded script but was not as yet producing cursive writing. It was the speed of delivery which was causing her most difficulty. Sarah has very good linguistic skills and could generate ideas quickly and easily but was frustrated with the difficulty of being able to translate her thoughts onto paper accurately.

Maths

Sarah does not present with any marked mathematical difficulties. She has a good basic understanding of mathematical computations and has acquired basic numeracy skills. She has been struggling a little with the acquisition of times tables and can be a little slow with mental maths, but in all other regards her maths functioning is a good average.

CONCLUSIONS

Sarah's presentation was that of a fairly classic student with dyslexia type or specific learning difficulties with no further significant complications. At this stage her level of difficulty was presenting within the mild range and given that appropriate remedial intervention was forthcoming it was likely that Sarah would make steady progress.

DISCUSSION POINTS

A diagnosis of dyslexia or specific learning difficulties at this comparatively early stage in a student's life is very fortunate as it is likely to lead to good remediation. In terms of expectations it would be expected that Sarah would achieve at least at an average level in terms of her literacy. While this may not be on a par with her general intellectual ability, she would be able to cope within the mainstream classroom. A key target with Sarah is to work on her specific learning issues until she is achieving at a good average level with most aspects of literacy skills. Sarah needs to understand the nature of her difficulties so as not to become unduly frustrated with her learning in class. She requires her teachers to appreciate her difficulties and make sure that her intellectual potential is not stifled as she progresses through her primary school years. Teachers need to be aware of her auditory processing issues and make sure that instructions are given very carefully to her and are actively reinforced where required.

RECOMMENDATIONS AND OUTCOMES

Sarah was placed on an appropriate remedial programme. She received one-to-one tuition from a specialist teacher who was trained to work with dyslexic students. She received two sessions of individual input per week. She was placed on a highly structured phonic-based programme delivered to her using multisensory methodology. Alongside this she worked on a daily practice programme to reinforce her ability to recognize and apply phonic strategies to reading and spelling. Further to this, the school recognized her learning difficulties. They provided support for her in the classroom in terms of further active rehearsal of word attack skills on a daily basis. She was heard to read regularly at school as well as at home. In terms of spelling and writing skills, Sarah began to learn and appreciate the etymology of words and look at word sums. She was encouraged to become much more observant of letter formations and encouraged to develop a cursive script.

Sarah was also recommended to contact either a Johansen IAS or TLP provider to establish whether this could support her learning. Sarah's parents were concerned about the diagnosis yet relieved by the recognition of her specific learning issues. They discussed the fact that dyslexia existed within their wider family. They were happy to be informed in detail about the nature of Sarah's learning potential and also her difficulties. They were happy to discuss the likely path of progress and learn about what to expect in terms of her rate of progress.

Sarah's teachers were a little surprised about Sarah's learning difficulties and began to readjust their expectations of her within the classroom environment. Her class teacher was particularly helpful in altering the ways in which she delivered instructions to Sarah and also by encouraging a higher level of active rehearsal of structured components of learning. She also helped by working independently with Sarah on her auditory memory problems. As a result Sarah became much more relaxed in class and was generally more attentive.

Sarah made steady progress during the course of the next two years at school with reading and spelling. She still lagged behind a little, particularly with spelling and writing, however when she was 9½ she began to take off with her reading and became much more independent as a learner.

JAMES (AGED 10)

REASON FOR REFERRAL

James's school teachers and parents were very concerned about his progress at school, both in terms of aspects of his learning and also in terms of his social integration. James was proving something of a mystery. He had initially settled well at school and seemed to be making good progress with his literacy-based skills, but had always struggled with aspects of maths. On a social level he was a quiet child who did not make great demands within the classroom and seemed a little anxious at times. As he had progressed through the years James had become increasingly agitated. He tended to drift in class and not always maintain good attention. At home

James presented as an anxious child who worried a lot about school. His parents were struggling to get him to school on a daily basis. Moreover, he kept having a number of illnesses which meant that he was away from school rather more than one would have liked. James read very well and did not present with reading or spelling issues. He did have some difficulties, however, with his handwriting and with his general presentation. A full assessment was requested to ascertain the nature of James's difficulties.

DEVELOPMENTAL HISTORY

James had been the subject of a very difficult, somewhat traumatic birth. He was born 4 weeks early; however he was not placed in a special care unit at this time. During early infancy he progressed well, however he was slow to attain physical developmental milestones and did not crawl. His language developed well. He was a reasonably articulate child from an early stage. As he progressed James had a further viral illness which required hospitalization. He was quite ill at this time and his parents were very concerned for him. Nevertheless, after a week in hospital he recovered extremely well. Other than this James did not present with any further significant medical issues during his early years. However, during the course of the last academic year James has begun to have a number of illnesses which have necessitated absence from school.

On a social front, James is happy and relaxed within his immediate family but has always been somewhat tentative outside of a small social grouping. He is regarded as a somewhat shy, anxious child.

James presents with some mild coordination issues, although this has never been formally addressed through medical services. He is a little clumsy at times and has difficulties with ball skills. He is very tentative in terms of climbing type activities and is not a 'risk taker' in terms of physical actions. He was slow to learn to ride a bike and still lacks confidence in this area.

At home James's level of concentration is reasonably good. He sits for a long time reading and engages in writing activities, although his presentation and handwriting skills are somewhat immature.

SCHOOL FACTORS

James has attended two schools during his early years. Initially he had demonstrated some separation anxiety and had struggled to cope in reception class (aged 4½). This lessened after about two months and he settled into his school routine. He began to read without any difficulty. Socially he tended to have singular friends but was generally amenable in class. Although he spoke well, James was not a particularly strong communicator within a social grouping, tending to be rather quiet and on the edge of groups. He did not like physical games with other students; however, he showed particular interest in the natural world and easily occupied himself with nature type activities.

As James progressed on to Years 2 and 3 he presented a similar profile. He was achieving at a satisfactory level in class, performing generally at a good average, his maths skills being slightly weaker than his literacy skills but nevertheless he was achieving reasonably comfortably. James's family then moved, causing a change of school for him. James again found it rather difficult to settle at his new school and to make friends. He was no trouble in class, being rather quiet and reserved and getting on with his work without demanding too much attention. His teachers were concerned about his social functioning and began to instigate some support to create friendships. Through this work James did latch on to one particular individual and they became quite close friends. The school were from this point reasonably happy with James's progress, however as he went into Year 5 (aged 10 years old), James began to show more difficulty at home. He was struggling to sleep well and was becoming increasingly anxious about going to school. He did have a number of genuine illnesses but he showed that he was slow to recover from these illnesses and tended to have odd days off. Following discussions between the parents and the school it was decided that an educational psychological assessment might be helpful in terms of understanding more about James and helping him to be more relaxed about school.

THE ASSESSMENT

At the point of assessment James was nervous and anxious. Time was spent with James alongside his family tracing his background details and engaging James in conversation with his family present. This did alter James's mood and he gradually relaxed. During the course of the individual assessment James was initially tentative in his responses, however, as we progressed through the tasks he relaxed greatly and began to open up and share some of his thoughts and feelings about himself and his life at school. In the event James really enjoyed the assessment. He felt it provided him with an opportunity to think through his difficulties and to begin to understand himself in more depth.

James proved to be an intriguing child to spend time with. He emerged as a somewhat socially shy individual who lacked confidence in his own abilities. He was very wary of critical comments and found aspects of school life very challenging.

Through the assessment James's level of concentration was excellent. He proved himself to be an exceptionally able child in terms of his verbal attributes but showed marked weaknesses with some of his performance test items. Nevertheless concentration was generally good throughout the assessment.

In terms of his language-based skills, James had no difficulties with understanding what was being said to him or with expressing his own responses. He formulated sentences well and had very good and extensive vocabulary. His lack of expression within the classroom was due to social inhibitors rather than any underlying language-based issues.

Cognitive factors

Verbal reasoning	Above average
Perceptual reasoning	Low average
Working memory	Above average
Speed of processing	Low average

James presented a very mixed cognitive profile. He showed a great deal of strength within the verbal system. Here he was functioning within the top 1 per cent of the general population, his verbal abilities being extremely competent. Moreover, he had very good general knowledge and had no difficulty with the retention of factual information.

James's weaknesses were with perceptual organization and speed of processing. Here he demonstrated marked spatial difficulties. He had further issues with his conceptual understanding of visual relationships.

James's strengths were in the following areas:

- verbal comprehension
- verbal reasoning
- vocabulary
- analytical thinking
- short-term memory skills.

James's weaknesses were in the following areas:

- spatial organization
- perceptual reasoning
- speed of processing.

Basic skills

Mathematical reasoning	Standard score 110
Word reading	Standard score 131
Comprehension	Standard score 130
Speed of processing	Standard score 115
Handwriting	16 wpm

James did not present with any reading difficulties, indeed his reading accuracy and comprehension, speed and fluency were all above average for his age. James's spelling level was presenting at an average for his age. The main issue for James in terms of his basic skills was with handwriting, his production of written work being rather difficult to decipher at times, his speed and fluency being average for his age.

With regard to maths skills, James is functioning at an average level for his age. He has good mental maths and had no difficulty with retention of times tables or with basic numeracy. He is experiencing more difficulties with higher level maths skills and is having some difficulty with interpreting graphs and with aspects of geometry.

Emotional factors

James undertook some self-assessment profiling with regard to his emotional issues. This revealed some marked difficulties with self-esteem and anxiety. He does not like criticism and would prefer to remain quiet in class rather than drawing attention to himself in any way. He was overly self-conscious and was anxious about other students' responses to him. He could be a little fixed in his thinking at times, particularly in relation to the actions of others towards him. He did appear to misjudge other people's intentions.

CONCLUSIONS

James is presenting as a complex student. He is exceptionally able within the verbal system but shows marked difficulties with aspects of non-verbal or performance functions, the discrepancies between these two areas being highly significant. Alongside this James has a history of coordination difficulties, his general profile therefore being suggestive of underlying dyspraxic issues. He is certainly having difficulties with the translation of thought to action. He is struggling with executive functions, that is, with processing, with organization and with execution of tasks.

His inherent issues are with coordination and perceptual difficulties which have not been diagnosed or recognized at an early stage in his development and the underlying coordination and perceptual issues are increasing levels of stress for him within the classroom and in social environments.

The most important thing for James is to learn and understand the nature of his own difficulties, to look at anxiety and how it affects him and also the relationship between stress and his presenting issues in terms of perceptual and spatial difficulties and speed of processing issues. Moreover, his coordination difficulties need further investigation to explore in depth the potential diagnosis of dyspraxia.

RECOMMENDATIONS AND OUTCOMES

The first step with James is to explain in detail to him the issues to hand in terms of his profile and presentation of difficulty, then to map out the way forward to help him overcome his difficulties. This needs to be discussed very sensitively with James so as to facilitate a positive self-esteem for him.

James's presentation is suggestive of dyspraxia. The next recommendation is for James to be assessed by an occupational therapist to examine the full nature and extent of his perceptual and coordination difficulties. Also, for recommendations to be made in terms of intervention and remediation.

In addition it was recommended for James to have an assessment from an INPP specialist to establish whether a neuro-developmental delay programme might be appropriate.

Within a classroom environment James requires his teachers to appreciate the complex nature of his difficulties but primarily to acknowledge his superior intellect particularly within the verbal system. Given that he is experiencing significant handwriting difficulties he needs some direct remedial intervention to help improve his posture in relation to handwriting and his letter formation.

Speed of processing is an issue for James. While he is able to take on board information verbally without any difficulty, he has problems with the speed at which he can produce written work. His verbal system works extremely quickly but he has a great deal of difficulty with structuring and organizing his thoughts onto paper efficiently. To assist with this he requires a study skills input delivered to him on an individual basis. He needs to learn how to brainstorm his ideas, how to structure and organize those ideas to produce competent essays. James is experiencing some mild difficulties with aspects of maths skills. He has good analytical thinking and reasonable facility with basic numeracy; however he struggles with more complex levels of maths. He needs further direct tutoring in this regard.

OUTCOME

James went on to be diagnosed with dyspraxia by an occupational therapist. Following assessment he also completed a neuro-developmental delay programme over the course of a year.

James was very perceptive and quick to understand the nature of the assessment and what it meant for him. The process helped him to discuss his own thoughts and feelings about his difficulties and this in itself began to alleviate some of his issues. Once he understood why he has difficulties translating his thoughts onto paper, he began to work more comprehensively to cope with his levels of anxiety. James still struggles with sport activities. He was diagnosed with dyspraxia and did undertake some remedial processes to help with balance and general coordination. However, it was mostly recommended that he should regularly engage in sporting activities of an individual type. James has always been somewhat reluctant in this regard and regularly needs to be encouraged by his family.

BEN (AGED 14)

REASON FOR REFERRAL

Ben was referred for a psychological assessment following school and parental concern about aspects of his behaviour at school and the general standard of his work outputs. Ben was perceived as a bright student. He is verbally competent and readily engages in discussion in class and at home. He seems to have a very good use of vocabulary. He has not presented with any marked specific learning issues in that he learned to read reasonably competently at an early stage. He has acquired at least average level of maths skills. He had no inherent difficulties with early mastery of times tables or with number bonds. The issue in terms of work production is with handwriting and presentation where he seems to lack care and attention. He rarely follows structures and guidelines provided for him by his teachers as to how to improve his general presentation and the quality of his written work.

In terms of behavioural factors, Ben has always presented with concentration and attention difficulties in class. This was not a significant problem for him in primary school. He was always regarded as being quite chatty and someone who did not always easily get down to a task but nevertheless he managed to achieve reasonably comfortably through primary school and it has only been since he began secondary education that Ben's level of difficulty has become more pronounced.

More recently, Ben has failed to hand in work on a regular basis and is falling behind with many assignments. Within the classroom he has been on a report card for disruptive behaviour. This intervention seemed to work for a short period of time but there were no sustained changes in Ben's way of operating within the classroom.

Information from Ben's tutor reveals that the school are feeling very frustrated with Ben. They perceive him as a bright, capable student who is not applying himself and is beginning now to under-achieve in a number of areas of the curriculum.

Ben's parents have become increasingly concerned about his behaviour at school. At home Ben is a happy-go-lucky, open and responsive student who is affectionate and by and large not particularly difficult to deal with and as yet there have not been any major discipline issues with Ben at home.

It should be noted that Ben's parents are separated. Their marriage dissolved when Ben was four years old. It was a reasonably amicable split and both of Ben's parents remain involved in his care on a regular basis.

DEVELOPMENTAL HISTORY

Ben was the result of a normal birth and delivery. He attained developmental milestones at appropriate times. He was a curious and interested baby who was described as being 'on the go' all the time. He did sleep reasonably well but was quite restless and would wake quickly and easily if any noises occurred. He would then be quite difficult to re-settle at night. He did not present with any particular feeding difficulties other than being a very fast eater. As a young child, Ben was very active and happiest when outdoors playing. He found it difficult to settle to tasks that required sustained levels of concentration and was not particularly adept at fine motor activities. He was, however, always a willing and cooperative student, being very friendly and affectionate.

Ben has not presented with any significant coordination difficulties. Indeed he has always been very adept at most sporting activities. He really enjoys rugby and plays for the school.

SCHOOL FACTORS

In terms of schooling, Ben was rather young in his year. He found it difficult to settle in his first class, particularly to tasks that required sustained levels of focus. He was very active and very chatty with other students. He did not, however, have any specific learning issues. He learned to read reasonably easily and generally achieved at an above average level in his year by the age of 7. As he progressed into the next class, he began to lose pace a little. Although he continued to read well his writing skills were less well developed and he showed weaknesses with spelling. He continued to progress satisfactorily with maths skills. Age 11, he achieved at an average level for English and maths and above average for science.

Initially Ben settled well into secondary school. He coped well with new social groupings and easily developed a friendship group. However, he did not cope particularly well with organizational factors in relation to operating successfully in secondary school. He was often forgetful of equipment that he needed for lessons and even sports equipment, even though he was very keen to undertake sports activities. Despite his teachers being very supportive in the first instance and then rather critical of him, his behaviour did not alter. Moreover, Ben began to struggle to hand in homework on time. His work presentation was always below expectations. Nevertheless Ben still had an endearing quality and many of his teachers thought warmly of him and regarded him as a student who was just struggling with organization. However, as he progressed through the next two years, his behaviour became somewhat more challenging within the classroom. He was very distracting to other students and would often be off task. He was never particularly confrontational with staff but nor would he readily follow instructions.

THE ASSESSMENT

Ben came very willingly to the assessment and readily engaged in all the tasks he was required him to perform. He was an articulate student who had no difficulty discussing the nature of his difficulties.

He swiftly responded to all the verbal items and had no difficulties in this area. He did, however, have more difficulty with tasks that required him to process information carefully and thoughtfully. He showed weaknesses with his analysis of visual information. When presented with a task that required considered, thoughtful responses, he had a tendency to be somewhat impulsive and this led to many careless errors on his part. Moreover, his ability to sustain his efforts when presented with complex, difficult tasks varied as we progressed through the assessment.

Cognitive factors

Verbal comprehension	Above average
Perceptual reasoning	Above average
Working memory	Above average
Speed of processing	Below average

These results indicated that Ben was generally functioning within the above average range of abilities. However, he demonstrated a marked discrepancy between the majority of his scores and his speed of processing, the latter being significantly weaker. Moreover, Ben was demonstrating issues with visual memory and with perceptual motor organization. These results were suggestive of underlying specific learning issues, particularly in relation to his weaknesses with spelling and writing skills.

Basic skills

Reading accuracy	Standard score 124
Reading comprehension	Standard score 128
Reading comprehension speed	Standard score 115
Spelling	Standard score 98
Handwriting speed	15 wpm

Ben clearly has no evident issues with reading. He reads very competently. He will undertake the process of reading for pleasure although he is not always inclined to do so due to a lack of patience on his part but he does not present with any other inherent reading issues. He has good auditory processing facility and no underlying phonological awareness issues.

Ben is showing some mild weaknesses with spelling skills. On testing he is performing within the average range, however, on observing his general written work there are more significant weaknesses within his spelling. Thus when Ben is writing at speed the quality of his spelling diminishes considerably. He often reverses letter sequences and omits or substitutes alternative letters. On the whole his offerings are close approximations to the word he is attempting to write and as such it is possible to decipher his offerings.

The main area of weakness for Ben is his handwriting skills. He produces a very sprawly script which mixes cursive writing with print. He is very unsettled when writing and tends to move his position. This causes a variation in the size and slope of his letters. When writing at length he begins to have some problems with his arm and he finds that his arm and hand ache considerably. He finds the process of writing at length rather uncomfortable and he lacks endurance on writing tasks.

Organizational factors

Although Ben is an able student the quality of his written work does not always reflect this. He shows marked difficulties with organising his thoughts onto paper in a well structured and organized fashion. Ben does let his ideas flow but in rather a random fashion, moreover he does not always go over his work to rearrange it or to check for spelling errors. Ben's issues with organization do extend to his written work in the above areas.

Ben has marked difficulties with his own organization in relation to his daily life. He often forgets things by his own admission; he is inconsistent in his application of strategies to assist himself with organizational factors and is aware that he frequently gets into trouble at school because of organizational issues. With regard to homework, he often fails to hand work in even though he has actually completed the task. This can be because he cannot find the work he has produced. It has been known for a piece of work to be in his bag but at the point of having to deliver it he is unable to find it in the bag. Ben is one of those students whose bag is always in a muddle and he never has any system for filing notes or keeping track of his work. When it comes to revision he has no decent notes to revise from.

Emotional/behavioural factors

Ben's profile was immediately suggestive of a student who has problems with organization, concentration and attention. He is very aware that he can be quite disruptive in class and that he can find it very difficult to get settled to tasks at times. Moreover, he has a significant level of insight into the nature of his own presentation at school and how he relates to other students. He feels that he is often waylaid by other students and even when he has tried in the past to refrain from unnecessary debate and discussion in class with his friends, he will find himself lapsing back into old habits very quickly, usually prompted by other students in the class from whom he finds it very difficult to detach himself.

During the course of the last academic year Ben was able to reveal that he has lost heart to some degree and is now beginning to give up. He feels that his attempts to try to improve his performance never succeed and even when he does try to produce reasonable work, his teachers never seem to recognize any of his efforts.

Ben meets the criteria for a possible diagnosis of attention deficit hyperactivity disorder.

CONCLUSIONS

Ben is a student of very good intellectual potential who is presenting with mild specific learning difficulties in relation to speed of processing. Alongside this he is presenting with mild ADHD. The two factors combined were causing Ben to have considerable levels of frustration within the classroom, to have difficulties with getting started on task and with his own personal organization.

Ben had always been a reasonably willing student. During the course of the last year his presentation has begun to alter as his teachers are beginning to be increasingly frustrated with him and are now passing on this frustration to Ben through an increased level of critical feedback. Ben's parents are also beginning to become more condemnatory of him in light of very negative school reports. These factors are all influencing Ben and he is generally now becoming quite angry and disaffected. Ben needs a significant amount of input in order to alter his chances at school.

First and foremost Ben needs considerable support to cope with workloads at school and to help him with his organization. To this end it was recommended that he had two sessions a week with a special needs teacher.

The aim of support work with Ben is primarily to organize his files, to help him more directly with his timetable and management of workload. It is also important that Ben receives direct help to get started on open-ended, unstructured tasks. Thus, any homework is discussed on a regular basis and Ben has clear direction as to how to accomplish tasks.

Ben's special needs teacher links with class subject teachers and carefully monitors Ben's concentration and performance in classes. On discussing this with his special needs teacher it was decided that one subject at a time should be targeted to help improve his performance. Given the compound nature of Ben's situation it would be unlikely that Ben could transform his performance in all aspects of his work in one fell swoop, thus one or two subjects are concentrated on initially and then he will gradually progress onto other subject areas. It was best to start with those subjects where Ben already had some positive feedback from teachers and where the subject teachers concerned were known to be particularly amenable to alterations in their own work style with Ben.

The special needs teacher links closely with Ben's family. Ben needs a good deal of support and backup at home, again to cope with workload, time management, organization, and in particular getting started on task.

On discussing the situation with his parents it was decided that Ben needs a fairly strict routine at home in terms of management of work and that he needs some supervision for work. Ben is the kind of student who would favour having a regular amount of time that he needed to set aside to work on schoolwork, that this is well timetabled and organized by his parents. If this routine is interrupted he completes more work tasks during the weekend.

In terms of organization, I discussed with Ben and his teachers the fact that Ben's level of organization is likely to be 2 or 3 years below expectations in terms of his current age, that it was also fair to assume that he could improve but he would be unable to do so without support and guidance. Time management with ADHD students is always a significant issue, thus I recommended having clocks in evidence both in his room and within the house that he regularly refers to. Similarly within his lessons, time factors are often noted. Ben needs a bag for school which is partly organized by his parents or whoever he is staying with at the time.

Within the classroom environment it can be very difficult to alter a child's behaviour, particularly when the peer group can often operate in a way so as to maintain a child's current presentation. Ben has changed his position within the classroom and sits at the front but to one side of the class, the teacher regularly interacts with him not in a punitive sense but by engaging him in dialogue and discussion about the work involved, support is always given at the beginning of a task to make sure that Ben can at least start on a task without difficulty.

Ben has some vulnerability in his self-esteem in relation to classroom factors. Individual teachers spend time with Ben discussing how he learns best and consider some alterations to management of work within the classroom on an individual basis.

If Ben gets drawn into conversation with other students the teacher tackles the other students first before necessarily homing in on Ben. Clearly, if Ben is out of order in the classroom then usual channels of discipline would apply, but he should not necessarily be the first person to challenge if others are involved.

Some suggestions were made around food items with Ben and it was discussed with his parents whether it might be useful for Ben to see a nutritionist about any possible food sensitivities. In the event many students with ADHD characteristics can benefit from eating slow release sugars very regularly through the school day. Part of the problem can be that the student does not eat sufficient amounts of food at any particular time and this was in fact the case with Ben. He was often skipping breakfast because he was rushed and in a hurry; he was snacking on inappropriate items such as crisps and biscuits, and at lunch time again not sitting for any length of time or eating a good lunch. This was discussed with all concerned and a new plan was put into place as to how to alter his regime.

A further area that was discussed with his family was the possibility of Ben seeking medication for his ADHD. If this route was to be taken up, Ben would need to seek further advice from medical specialists, either a psychiatrist or a consultant paediatrician. In the event Ben's parents decided not to opt for this route. They were more interested in applying many of the recommendations listed above; however it was felt important to review Ben's progress in six months to see whether or not that particular course of action was required.

OUTCOME

During the course of the last two years Ben has made steady progress. He has not completely transformed and remains a very lively, bubbly child who is quite difficult to settle at times. He can be very chatty and a little disruptive in class but his attitude has altered and he remains now a positive natured child who many of his teachers have a lot of affection for. He is achieving reasonably well, although is not yet quite meeting expectations in terms of his intellectual potential.

Ben still has persistent organizational difficulties. He sticks to the schemes organized for him within the family and has found it particularly beneficial that his parents are working together in terms of managing his performance at home. However, he still forgets things. Even when they are placed on the table for him he can walk out of the door without certain items that he requires. The positive is that teachers no longer get frustrated or irritated by this, he merely has to back-track at some point and make sure that he hands things in as frequently as possible.

He has benefited greatly from special needs support. Regular coaching on organizational factors has proved enormously beneficial for him. He has a very good relationship with his special needs teacher who mediates for him when there are any issues with any individual teachers. Ben still finds it very difficult to settle to work tasks independently and still needs quite a lot of backup, but he is responsive to receiving this backup and does not resist help.

Ben's level of anger has diminished and it no longer causes him difficulties at school. He is positive about his achievements and does feel that he will continue on to study. He now has a greater level of understanding of his own frustrations and is beginning to feel calmer when having to work. He understands that in order to pay attention to detail and accuracy he has to work slowly. While he still finds this inherently frustrating, he is beginning to manage this process more directly and is much less agitated now when working. He has discovered that the use of headphones and listening to certain types of music can be particularly helpful for him when he is studying independently.

Final thoughts

Every child has a different story. They cannot easily be labelled, categorized or packaged in simple terms. It is possible, through careful analysis, to provide explanations for the child's presenting problems that will allow for appropriate intervention to ensue.

It can be hard for teachers and parents to locate the cornerstone of a child's difficulties. Even if they able to do so, the child might be locked into patterns of learning or behaving that perpetuate his difficulties. For change to occur the child himself has to actually believe he has the potential and capability to change and improve his performance.

Children's problems are often compound and multifaceted. It can be hard to locate the crux of the matter and strip away the layers that cloud the situation. An assessment can be cathartic for the child and lead him to have a better understanding of his own strengths and weaknesses which in itself can promote change.

The overall analysis of the child's individual situation and difficulties might include diagnostic labels, classifications and ability measures. These are helpful as they provide legitimate explanations for the child's presenting problems. They often serve to remove blame from the equation and help to modify expectations. They can also help to attribute patterns of behaviour and learning styles and give clear direction for remedial interventions. They can also provide a shorthand language to help all those involved with the child have a common understanding of the needs of the child concerned.

Even when the difficulties that a child has are evident, it is a complex issue to design and implement an appropriate remedial programme particularly when the child has many differing needs to be addressed.

Clarity needs to be given to the range of presenting problems while at the same time giving clear directives as to where to direct efforts to best produce change.

The role of the educational psychologist is in part to clarify issues, to help expose, disentangle and eradicate blocks to learning and to provide guidance to enable further steps towards progress, thereby providing the climate for change.

Any programme of intervention for the child requires steadfast commitment from the professionals, parents and the child himself, as well as time, resources and expertise. Given this, remediation needs to be appropriately targeted. The assessment can serve to bring parties involved together and focus their efforts in a supportive manner. When this occurs the child often makes rapid progress. If the child doesn't see some change quickly he will often lose heart and give up.

A common factor to all three case studies was the misperceptions about the individuals concerned and their ability learn and to adapt. The intervention from the educational psychologist serves to challenge these presumptions and to facilitate alterations in thinking, behaviour and emotions that will allow the child to blossom.

The case studies described are purposefully disparate so as to demonstrate the range and complexity of children's difficulties as they present at school. They do, however, illustrate the following:

1. Early assessment and identification of difficulties prevents compound emotional and behavioural issues.

2. Early developmental factors can have lasting implications for a child's social and academic performance and need to be identified and tackled appropriately.

3. Individually tailored interventions are required according to the nature of each case.

4. Treatment needs to be specific in nature, delivered on a frequent basis by knowledgeable and suitably qualified practitioners.

5. Children thrive when they have awareness and understanding of their own abilities as well as their blocks to learning.

6. Children can adapt and overcome complex difficulties given that they have appropriate guidance and support.

Kids Can Succeed Record Form

Pupil's name:
Date of birth:
Person completing this form and relationship to child:
Date record started:

Section one
Ask people who know the child well what the child's strengths and areas of concern are. Ask the child as well if appropriate.

Strengths	Areas of concern
	.

Section two
Use the checklists by ticking, highlighting and making notes. Attach copies and summarize below.

Checklists used (include dates)	Comments
	.

Section three
Use this section to summarize any reports, meetings and information from health professionals.

Professional (include dates)	Comments
	.

Section four
Other information.

Section five
Details of subsequent discussions with school/others.

Date and people present	Notes and action points: what will happen next and by what date?

Rhymes, Rhythm and Movement

Singing, finger play, music skills, physical activity and having fun playing together are great ways to develop all aspects of learning. Here are just a couple of examples of activities to share.

Over the Ocean

This is a very simple activity, but it is very good for both physical development and for helping children to learn sequences.

Pre-teach the actions. This seems like such a simple activity, but it can be surprisingly difficult for the young children to master.

Children roll one arm over the other (roly poly arms) in a forward direction for the first part.

For 'jellyfish', put fingertips together and push palms together and apart in a rhythmical fashion to simulate a jellyfish swimming.

Repeat the rhyme, rolling forearms backwards.

For the second verse, for 'starfish', make hands into fists then open wide quickly twice.

Over the Ocean

Over the ocean, over the sea,

Catching jellyfish for my tea.

Over the ocean, over the sea,

Catching starfish just for me.

I Hide My Hands by Marlene Rattigan[6]

Marlene Rattigan's books are an excellent resource and, as they each come with CDs, they are a complete programme.

This activity helps with fine motor coordination, memory of sequences, body awareness and directionality. Follow the movement instructions in the song and in brackets.

I Hide My Hands

I hide my hands (*put them behind your back*)

I shake my hands

I give a little clap

I shake my hands

I hide them in my lap

I creep my hands (*walk fingers up the body*)

I crawl my hands

Right up to my nose

I creep my hands

I crawl my hands

Way down to my toes

---

6   Marlene Rattigan is the author of *Kidz-Fiz-Biz: Physical Business for Children* (2004). She is an early childhood teacher working in Australia. She runs workshops internationally and her movement programme is designed for 2–7 year olds.

Central Auditory Processing Disorders Leaflet

This information is useful for teachers and others working in schools, regardless of whether there are children with specific learning needs. By stressing the importance of multisensory teaching and communication, they make learning more effective.

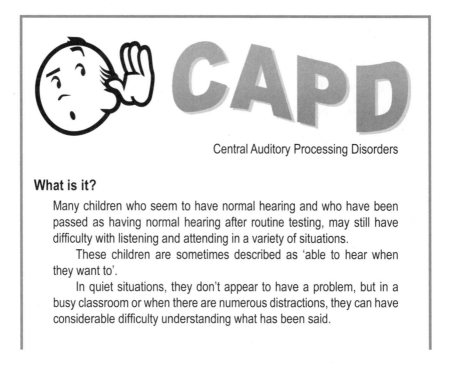

Central Auditory Processing Disorders

What is it?

Many children who seem to have normal hearing and who have been passed as having normal hearing after routine testing, may still have difficulty with listening and attending in a variety of situations.

These children are sometimes described as 'able to hear when they want to'.

In quiet situations, they don't appear to have a problem, but in a busy classroom or when there are numerous distractions, they can have considerable difficulty understanding what has been said.

Problems they can experience

- Hearing speech clearly against a background of noise
- Picking out one voice from others
- Identifying where a voice or sound is coming from
- Hearing speakers clearly at a distance
- Listening selectively to one side or the other

They may also have difficulty:

- Maintaining attention to speakers
- Remembering spoken messages or instructions
- Recognising letter sound in isolation
- Combining letter sounds to make words
- Breaking words down into their component sounds

What we can do to help them in their everyday communication

- Gain attention

  Ensure the child is attending before giving instructions, e.g.

  ○ call their name and ask them to look at you

  ○ refocus the child's attention

- Break down instructions

  Help the child to follow by presenting information in small, manageable steps. Reduce the complexity of the message in terms of type of vocabulary and grammar used.

- Use visual aids

  Assist the child's understanding, memory and sequencing skills by writing key words and instructions on the board.

  It may also be helpful to provide simple pictures to clarify activities, use visual clues such as gestures and utilize mind maps.

- Check understanding

  Ask the child questions or ask them to explain the task to check they understand. Encourage the child to indicate when they have not understood and consider ways to help them successfully follow instructions.

- Plan, do and review

  Prepare the child by explaining what you are going to do and what materials you will be using. During activities, use related vocabulary and describe your own or the child's actions. After the activities, encourage the child to participate in discussion about the sequence of events.

- Repeat

  Be repetitive when talking, particularly for new vocabulary and concepts. Say it once, pause and repeat it exactly, as the child may need time to process the information. You may need to rephrase, or explain information in a different way.

- Provide breaks

  A break will ideally involve a physical activity, thereby utilising the other side of the brain to that used for a language task. Previous material can then be reviewed after a break, with the advantage of their improved attention span.

- Be supportive

  Be supportive to the child and praise them for the attempts they make to follow and participate in the classroom.

Advice to teachers on ways to reduce unnecessary classroom noise

Reducing background noise

- Try to keep classroom 'chatter' to a minimum when teaching or giving information and instructions

- Do not give out important information when the children are 'on the move', e.g. at the end of a lesson or whilst re-organising themselves into working groups

- Investigate the noise levels given out by water pipes, blow heaters or air conditioners and reduce the levels when possible or replace with quiet equipment, e.g. radiators instead of blow heaters

- Put measures into practice to reduce noise levels if there are 'staggered' lesson change-over periods

- Use 'soft-top' desks and tables

- Seal unused doors/openings between classrooms

- Carpet all classrooms apart from one area for wet or messy activities
- If carpeting is impossible fit 'rubber shoes', to desks and chairs
- Fit double glazing to windows if fronting a busy road or an area of high noise levels

Reducing reverberation

- Carpet all classrooms apart from one area for wet or messy activities
- Put blinds or curtains on windows
- Fit pin boards or soft material to all hard wall areas
- Fit acoustic tiles on ceilings

General considerations

- Listeners hear better if they are close to a speaker
- Teachers should look at a pupil when speaking to them
- Regular checks should be made to ensure that the pupil understands and is not being 'left behind'
- If possible seat the pupil next to an able pupil who can help when listening/understanding has broken down
- Written support by way of handouts or bullet points on the board can be very helpful.

Personal sound-field systems (a mini public address system where the teacher has a microphone and the pupil a small speaker on the desk) can be helpful for pupils wlth CAPD.

If you suspect that a child you know has CAPD

Teachers

- Talk to parents
- Talk to other teachers
- Talk to the school nurse

Parents

- Go to family doctor or school nurse and request referral to Audiology

School nurse

- Refer to Audiology

Leaflet compiled by the following Multi-disciplinary team:

1. Educational Psychologist: Tom Williams (Reading LEA)

2. Speech and Language Therapists: Kristin Broadbridge (King Edward VII Hospital, Windsor) and Julia Kidd (Royal Berkshire Hospital, Reading)

3. Educational Audiologist: Nerys Roberts (Sensory Consortium Service)

4. Paediatrician: Dr Dorothy Milne (St Mark's Hospital, Maidenhead)

5. Audiologist: Lize Pretorius (King Edward VII)

Useful Resources

Auditory

AFASIC: Unlocking Speech and Language
1st Floor
20 Bowling Green Lane
London
EC1R 0BD
Phone: 020 7490 9410
Helpline: 08453 555577 (Monday to Friday 10.30 am–2.30 pm)
Website: www.afasic.org.uk
This site provides information and training for parents and professionals and produces a range of publications.

Association of Speech and Language Therapists in Independent Practice (ASLTIP)
Website: www.helpwithtalking.com
ASLTIP has two main functions: 1) to provide information on independent speech and language therapy throughout the United Kingdom, and 2) to support speech and language therapists in independent practice.

Auditory Integration Training
Website: www.drguyberard.com

I Can
Website: www.ican.org.uk
I Can is a children's communication charity that aims to provide help for all children and young people who struggle to communicate properly so that they can have a happy childhood, make progress at school and thrive as adults.

Integrated Listening Systems
Website: www.integratedlistening.com
Integrated Listening Systems® (iLs®) provides training and equipment that improves physical and mental aptitude.

Johansen IAS
Website: www.johansenias.com

Listening Fitness
Website: www.listeningfitness.com
Listening Fitness is an educational technique that uses pre-recorded music, rich in high frequency, and our own voice to develop, improve and enrich listening skills.

The Listening Programme
Website: www.learning-solutions.co.uk

Samonas Auditory Stimulation
Website: www.samonas.com

Talking Point
Website: www.talkingpoint.org.uk
This site contains lots of great information to support children's speech and language.

Therapeutic Listening
Website: www.advancedpediatrictherapies.com

Tomatis Method
Website: www.tomatis-group.com

Books

Parsons, S. and Branagan, A. (2005) *Language for Thinking: A Structured Approach for Young Children*. Oxon: Speechmark.

Peer, L. (2005) *Glue Ear: An Essential Guide for Teachers, Parents and Health Professionals*. London: David Fulton Publishers.

Dyslexia, dyspraxia and ADHD

Australian Dyspraxia Foundation
Website: www.dyspraxia.com.au

British Dyslexia Association
Unit 8 Bracknell Beaches
Old Bracknell Lane
Bracknell
RG12 7BW
Tel: 0845 251 9003
Fax: 0845 251 9005
National Helpline: 0845 251 9002
Website: www.bdadyslexia.org.uk

Canadian Dyslexia Association
Website: www.dyslexiaassociation.ca

Dyslexia Action
Park House
Wick Road
Egham
Surrey
TW20 0HH
Phone: 01784 222 300
Email: info@dyslexiaaction.org.uk
Website: www.dyslexiaaction.org.uk

Dyslexia Foundation of New Zealand
Website: www.dyslexiafoundation.org.nz

Dyspraxia Foundation
This site has many useful national and international links.
8 West Alley
Hitchin
Hertfordshire
SG5 1EG
Helpline: 01462 454 986
Email: dyspraxia@dyspraxiafoundation.org.uk
Website: www.dyspraxiafoundation.org.uk

Dyspraxia USA
Website: www.dyspraxiausa.org

International Dyslexia Association
Website: www.interdys.org

LD Online
Website: www.ldonline.org
An international website that provides information and advice about learning disabilities and ADHD.

Learning Disabilities Association of America
Website: www.ldanatl.org

National Attention Deficit Disorder Association
Website: www.add.org

Learning support

Department for Education (formerly DCSF)
You can get copies of the Special Educational Needs Code of Practice and a list of other useful DCSF (Department for Children, Schools and Families) documents from the DCSF website at www.teachernet.gov.uk/wholeschool/sen or from DCSF Publications Centre on 0845 6022260
Many publications are available in a number of languages such as Bengali, Cantonese and Urdu.

Institute for Neuro-Physiological Psychology (INPP)
Gives worldwide information and contacts.
1 Stanley Street
Chester
CH1 2LR
Tel/Fax: 01244 311414
Website: www.inpp.org.uk

Learning Connections
Website: www.learningconnections.com.au

Move to Learn
Website: www.movetolearn.com.au
This website features an interactive test that will help to provide an idea about the areas that most need attention in your student/child/self.

Schooldays
Website: www.schooldaysmagazine.com
An online education magazine for parents and schools, written by specialists in their fields in education from Australia, New Zealand, USA, UK and Canada.

Screen Learning
Website: www.screenlearning.com
Screen Learning produces diagnostic assessment tools to help identify a child's strengths and support early interventions. This is done via online games for children that are then scored, leading to a feedback form and profile which clearly shows how well a child is performing in key areas of early learning.

Visual

Australian College of Behavioural Optometry
Website: www.acbo.org.au

British Association of Behavioural Optometrists
Website: www.babo.co.uk

Canadian Association of Optometrists
Website: www.opto.ca

Optometric Extension Programme Foundation (USA)
Website: www.oepf.org

References

Adler, P.M. (2009) 'What is Behavioural Optometry?' Optometric Vision Therapy Course OVT-1A, St Albans, 31 May 2009.

Allen, M. (1996) 'Prematurity.' In A. Capute and P. Accardo (eds) *Developmental Disabilities in Infancy and Childhood* (second edition). Maryland: Paul H. Brookes Publishing Co.

Barrett, B.T. (2008) 'A critical evaluation of the evidence supporting the practice of behavioural vision therapy.' Ophthalmic and Physiological Optics 29, 1, 4–25.

Beaver, M., Brewster, J., Jones, P., Keene, A., Neaum, S. and Tallack, J. (1994) *Babies and Young Children: Book 1 Development 0-7.* Cheltenham: Stanley Thornes.

Beckerleg, T. (2009) *Fun with Messy Play.* London and Philadelphia: Jessica Kingsley Publishers.

Beever, S. (2009) *Happy Kids, Happy You.* Carmarthen: Crown House Publishing.

Bellis, J. T. (2002) *When the Brain Can't Hear.* New York: Atria Books.

British Society of Audiology (2007) 'Auditory Processing Disorder Steering Committee Interim Position Statement on APD.' Available at www.thebsa.org.uk/apd, accessed 30 September 2010.

Cheatum, B.A. and Hammond, A.A. (2000) *Physical Activities for Improving Children's Learning and Behaviour: A Guide to Sensory Motor Development.* Leeds: Human Kinetics.

Christmas, J. (2009) *Hands on Dyspraxia.* Bucks: Speechmark Publishing.

Coulter, D.J. (1995) 'Music and the making of the mind.' *Early Childhood Connections: The Journal of Music and Movement-Based Learning, Winter.*

Couperous, J.W. and Nelson, C.A. (2008) 'Early Brain Development and Plasticity.' In K. McCartney and D. Phillips (eds) *Blackwell Handbook of Early Childhood Development.* Oxford: Blackwell Publishing.

Curran, A. (2008) *The Little Book of Big Stuff about the Brain.* Carmarthen: Crown House Publishing.

Doidge, N. (2007) *The Brain That Changes Itself: Stories of Personal Triumph from the Frontiers of Brain Science.* London: Penguin.

Eliot, L. (1999) *What's Going on in There? How the Brain and Mind Develop in the First Five Years of Life.* New York: Bantam Books.

Gilmor, T.M. (1999) 'The efficacy of the Tomatis Method for children with learning and communication disorders.' *International Journal of Listening 13*, 12–23.

Glover, V. (2002) 'Effects of antenatal stress and anxiety.' *British Journal of Psychiatry 180*, 389-391.

Goddard Blythe, S.A. (2002) *Reflexes, Learning and Behaviour: A Window into a Child's Mind.* Oregon: Fern Ridge Press.

Goddard Blythe, S.A. (2004) *The Well-Balanced Child.* Stroud: Hawthorn Press.

Goddard Blythe, S.A. (2005) 'Releasing Intelligence Through Movement: A Survey of Individual Studies Carried Out Using the INPP Programme for Schools.' The 17th European Conference of Neuro-Developmental Delay in Children with Specific Learning Difficulties, Edinburgh, 19–20 March 2005.

Goddard Blythe, S.A. (2008) 'Developmental Readiness: The Foundation for Later Learning Success.' The Open Eye Seminar, British Association for Early Childhood, London, 4 October 2008.

Goddard Blythe, S.A. (2009) *Attention, Balance and Coordination: The ABC of Learning Success.* Chichester: Wiley-Blackwell.

Goswami, U. (2008) Foresight Mental Capital and Wellbeing Project. *Learning Difficulties: Future Challenges.* London: The Government Office for Science.

Institute for Neuro-Physiological Psychology (2009) 'One Day Training Courses for Teachers in the use of the INPP Schools' Programme.' Available at www.inpp.org.uk/special_needs_training/one_day.php, accessed 28 September 2010.

International Dyslexia Association (2007) 'How do people "get" dyslexia?' Available at www.interdys.org/FAQHowDoPeopleGet.htm, accessed 28 September 2010.

Kurtz, L.A. (2006) *Visual Perception Problems in Children with AD/HD, Autism, and other Learning Disabilities: A Guide for Parents and Professionals.* London and Philadelphia: Jessica Kingsley Publishers.

Leeds, J. (2001) *The Power of Sound.* Vermont: Healing Arts Press.

Lyytinen, H. *et al.* (2008) 'Early Identification and Prevention of Dyslexia: Results From a Prospective Follow-up Study of Children at Familial Risk of Dyslexia.' In G. Reid, A. Fawcett, F. Manis and L. Siegel (eds) *The Sage Book of Dyslexia.* London: Sage Publications.

Medwell, J. Strand, S. and Wray, D. (2008) 'The links between handwriting and composing for Year 6 children.' *The Times Educational Supplement,* 17 October 2008.

Meggitt, C. (2006) *Child Development: An Illustrated Guide. Birth to 16 years.* Harlow: Heinemann.

Mellilo, R. and Leisman, G. (2004) *Neurobehavioural Disorders of Childhood: An Evolutionary Perspective.* New York: Kluwer Academic/Plenum Publications.

Mental Health Foundation (2000) 'Attention Deficit Hyperactivity Disorder (ADHD).' Available at www.mentalhealth.org.uk/information/mental-health-a-z/adhd/?locale=en, accessed 28 September 2010.

Millodot, M. (2000) *A Dictionary of Optometry and Visual Science* (fifth edition). Oxford: Butterworth-Heinemann.

Miranda, R.A. and Ullman, M.T. (2007) 'Double dissociation between rules and memory in music – an event-related potential study.' *Neuroimage 38*, 331–345.

Molfese, D. *et al.* (2008) 'Familial Predictors of Dyslexia: Evidence from Pre-School Children with and Without Familial Dyslexia Risk.' In G. Reid, A. Fawcett, F. Manis and L. Siegel (eds) *The Sage Book of Dyslexia*. London: Sage Publications.

Mountstephen, M. (2010) *Meeting Special Needs: A Practical Guide to Support Children with Speech, Language and Communication Needs*. London: Practical Pre-School Books.

MRC Institute of Hearing Research (2004) 'What is Auditory Processing Disorder?' Available at www.infosheets.apduk.org/whatapd.htm, accessed 30 September 2010.

Palmer, S. (2007) *Toxic Childhood: How the Modern World is Damaging Our Children and What We Can Do About It*. London: Orion Health.

Palmer, S. (2009) *21st Century Boys: How Modern Life is Driving Them Off the Rails and What We Can Do to Get Them Back on Track*. London: Orion.

Panksepp, J. (2007) 'Can Play Diminish ADHD?' *Journal of the Canadian Academy of Child and Adolescent Psychiatry 16*, 2, 57–66.

Pheloung, B. (2004) 'Move to learn: neurological maturity leading to academic readiness.' Sixth British Dyslexia Association International Conference, University of Warwick, 27–30 March 2004.

Pheloung, B. (2006) *School Floors*. Sydney: Iceform.

Phillips, D.P. (2007) 'An Introduction to Central Auditory Neuroscience.' In F.E. Musiek and G.D. Chermak (eds) *Handbook of (Central) Auditory Processing Disorder*, Vol.1. San Diego: Pleural Publishing.

Rattigan, M. (2004) *Kidz-Fiz-Biz: Physical Business for Children – Learning through Drama, Dance and Song*. Carmarthen: Crown House Publishing.

Ratey, J. and Hagerman, E. (2008) *Spark: The Revolutionary New Science of Exercise and the Brain*. New York: Little Brown and Company.

Richardson, A. (2006) *They Are What You Feed Them: How Food Can Improve Your Child's Behaviour, Mood and Learning*. London: Harper Thorsons.

Rose, J. (2009) *Identifying and Treating Children and Young People with Dyslexia and Literacy Difficulties*. London: Department for Children, Schools and Families. Available at http://publications.education.gov.uk/eOrderingDownload/00659-2009DOM-EN.pdf, accessed 28 September 2010.

Snowling, M.J., Muter, V. and Carroll, J. (2007) 'Children at family risk of dyslexia: a follow-up in early adolescence.' *Journal of Child Psychology and Psychiatry 48*, 609-618.

Sousa, D. (2007) *How the Special Needs Brain Learns* (second edition). Thousand Oaks, CA: Corwin Press.

White, H. and Evans, C. (2005) *Learning to Listen to Learn: Using Multisensory Teaching for Effective Listening*. London: Paul Chapman Publishing.

Index